MORE
GOLDEN OAK

Velma Susanne Warren

4880 Lower Valley Road, Atglen, PA 19310 USA

Dedication

To the Mighty Oak Tree, who lives on in this furniture.

WHITE OAK

Credits:

"The Oak Tree Logo," found on p. 4, is owned by the Calvary Fellowship Church, Downingtown, Pennsylvania, and is used with their permission.

"The Story of the Wood," © 1993 Pamela Cardullo. From *Beyond the Gate,* TERRA NOVA, page 5.

Copyright © 1998 by Velma Susanne Warren
Library of Congress Catalog Card Number: 98-86444

Designed by Bonnie M. Hensley
Layout by Randy L. Hensley
Typeset in Bookman/Times New Roman

ISBN: 0-7643-0645-6
Printed in China
1 2 3 4

Published by Schiffer Publishing Ltd.
4880 Lower Valley Road
Atglen, PA 19310
Phone: (610) 593-1777; Fax: (610) 593-2002
e-mail: schifferbk@aol.com
Please write for a free catalog.
This book may be purchased from the publisher.
Please include $3.95 for shipping.

In Europe, Schiffer books are distributed by
Bushwood Books
6 Marksbury Avenue
Kew Gardens
Surrey TW9 4JF England
Phone: 44 (0)181 392-8585; Fax: 44 (0)181 392-9876
e-mail: bushwd@aol.com

Please try your bookstore first.

We are interested in hearing from authors
with book ideas on related subjects.

Contents

Acknowledgments

I wish to extend my appreciation to all those who have so wonderfully supported my efforts during the creation of this book.

"Thank you" to my friends and family, my antique dealer buddies, my customer friends and acquaintances, near and far, and my Downingtown Mainstreet buddies, who visit the Oak Emporium Antiques to see the latest oak arrivals.

"Thank You" to Bill Brooks of Acorn Classics, Kingwood, Texas, for contributing numerous photographs of selected pieces from his prized personal collection. He has enabled us to see items that have never been seen. Feast your eyes.

Also, contributing to this collection are:

E. J. Cole, Cole's Antique Village, Pearland, Texas; J. DiScala, Private Collector, Downingtown, Pennsylvania; R. Ferguson of Ferguson Antiques, Pottstown, Pennsylvania; R. and J. Hoopes, Private Collector, Buford, Georgia; G. Pennington of Gary Pennington Antiques, Downingtown, Pennsylvania; R. and E. Rhoads, Auctioneer, Douglasville, Pennsylvania; D. Sadler of Collector's Corner, Downingtown, Pennsylvania; R. and G. Shafer of Shafer's Antiques, Gilbertsville, Pennsylvania; M. & J. Sharp, Private Collector, Glenmoore, Pennsylvania; C. Wise, Malvern, Pennsylvania.

Thank you to Pam Cardullo for writing "The Story of the Wood" and to Springton Manor Farm for being nearby.

"....will be like a tree planted..."
—Psalm 1:1-3

Preface

The Story of the Wood

by Pam Cardullo

Respect the wood, as it has swelled,
with every drop of rain that fell
And, it has shrunk again with every sun that rises.
In the building of its rings it tells of joy and suffering
It marks the prophesy for man and writes the history of the land

Respect the eye that chose this tree beneath the forest canopy
It was the last eye to see it in its glory
It knew the tale the wood would tell,
but could not speak until it fell
It chose this story for ourselves like a good book off the shelf

Chorus:
The story of life's seasons is the ballad that it sings
Our lives are marked and bound together by concentric rings

Respect the arm and simple strength that subdued
its mighty length
That embraced the wood with metal, bone, and muscle
More than life came crashing down as one more giant hit
the ground

And was carted to the mill
Somewhere the stump will mourn it still

Respect the labor and the toil; of those who took this fruit of soil
And sliced it into slabs and planks and lumber
Those that stacked it in the yard, those who shipped
it wide and far
Did they know where it would land as they held
it in their hand?

Respect the heart and mind that conceived a new design
That would bring together disparate slabs of timber
To rebuild the tree anew in a form both me and you
Could appreciate in awe what God's eye alone once saw

Last of all respect the hand that took these pieces and this plan
And added skill and art and all that it was able
The hand that chiseled, carved and planed, that sanded once
and twice again—
And now the story of the wood is more clearly understood
As it speaks to us through this chair and table.

The Queen Penn Oak. *"Respect the wood, as it has swelled, with every drop of rain that fell."*

Farmland Monarch—The sign in front of the Queen Penn Oak: "When William Penn arrived in Philadelphia, in 1682, the Queen oak you are standing in front of was just an acorn. Three hundred years later ... this tree's trunk has grown to over 16 feet around.

"Her partner, the larger King Penn Oak is on your right, by the pond, and is 18 feet, 9 inches around. If these trees could talk, you would hear the entire history of Springton Manor Farm.

"This magnificent pair of white oaks are fortunate to live outside the forest, enabling them to spread their branches into huge canopies of leaves. Forest oaks remain compact due to their competition for sunlight."

Credit: *Nature Trail Brochure.* Springton Manor Farm, Springton Road, Glenmoore, PA 19343.

Beyond the gate, is a 300 acre farm acquired in 1980 by the Board of Commissioners of Chester County, Pennsylvania. It is operated as a demonstration farm and is open to the public. All are welcome to visit.

The King Penn Oak. *"Respect the eye that chose this tree beneath the forest canopy."*

"Respect the heart and mind that conceived a new design." Entirely quartersawn, this Danner 68-inch tall revolving bookcase is 33 inches by 25 inches deep on each side; internal height is 52 inches. Squarely constructed of three stacking sections with lift-up glass doors on two sides and recessed panels with fold-down writing tables on the opposite sides. Sits on a revolving stand. $3000-$4000.

There's the stump of a once grand oak just behind the dedication plaque.

Of quality and reverence, this solid quartersawn alter table carries its inscription: *"In Remembrance of Me."* $900-$1000.

Concentric rings show their patterns, as they travel across the side of this small blanket chest. This chest is perfect coffee-table size. *"Our lives are...bound together by concentric rings."*

Quartersawn tiger stripes radiate on this small suitcase; 13 inches by 24 inches by 8 inches deep—it was once sold filled with tools.

Known as "The King's Chair" to those who have seen it, this magnificent armchair speaks for itself. Sloping arms flow from the shoulders rolling into handrests. Shapely legs with large, carved claw feet support this regal seat. $1700-$1900.

Detail of King's Chair. Elegant from the rear, as well.

Detail of King's Chair. Notice the deeply carved crest.

Large, bulbous, twisted legs support this outstanding library writing desk. Fine carvings and tiny beading decorate its beveled edge. A drawer at each end is concealed within the contoured apron, visible only by the brass ring drawer pulls. Designed for the use of two, perhaps an Emeralite double desk lamp sat in the middle, giving light to both scholars as they wrote. $1500-$1800.

Detail of library writing desk.

Detail of library writing desk. S-curls support the shelf. Five-toed claw feet are scaled with well defined toenails.

9

In Praise of the Oak

For strength and durability, no wood has endured through the centuries like oak. It has no rivals. It is quite a tree! It is everywhere. It shows up from barn rafters to choir stalls, in windmills, water mills, barrels, boats, floors, and, of course, home furnishings. It is everywhere!

The plentiful oak forests of 1900 have all come down. Conservation of trees was not of importance at that time. Vast quantities of lumber were milled without regard to waste. Piles of sawdust resulted from quartersawing the oak for its transformation into furniture.

It was not until approximately 1915 that anyone noticed the thinning forests. At that time, conservation efforts were made by saving the best lumber for veneer, which was applied to furniture constructed of lesser quality lumber. The quality, solid quartersawn construction of the past disappeared.

A century later, great quantities of this furniture have traveled through years of disregard and neglect, to rise to the status of "heirloom." No other furniture possesses the "life" found in the oak grain nor the beauty and intrigue found in the endless variety of styles and designs that were made yesterday and sought-after today.

As the twenty-first century approaches, we live in a world of high-speed electronic technology, but look who's here. It's the "Stork."

The quartersawn, beautifully hand-carved stork awaits his time to deliver the new century. Standing 45 inches tall with his detailed wings in full view, he stands on a 17-inch square platform and balances a 21-inch square top upon his head. So sweet he is. $5000-$6000.

Introduction

The majority of the items shown in this collection have crossed my path, in view of my camera, during the past several years. They have been gathered, restored, photographed, and have found new homes with new families; far and near.

Many items are shown in refinished condition, but needed little or no repair when purchased. A new finish applied, mirrors resilvered, and brasses polished, that's all. Hardware including drawer pulls, escutcheons, knobs, hat hooks, etc., are entirely original on every item shown. Some are beauties in themselves.

Immaculate original finish means pristine and well-preserved as when the item was new. Old or darkened varnish means deteriorated original finish, otherwise good condition.

Regarding the prices which are determined by size, design and most importantly condition, a particular item is worth whatever a particular individual is willing to pay on any particular day.

As time goes on, items are collected, the quantity available for purchase diminishes, the demand increases and so do the prices. One collector decides to part with an item and the next collector wants it enough to pay the asking price. And so it goes.

Now, is the time to appreciate the wood; the beauty and durability contained therein. Purchase the best items that you can, as soon as you can. Everlasting enjoyment will be your return.

Oak tall case hall clock; 98 inches tall, solid quartersawn. Nine-day German clock movement. Brass face displays its roman numeral hour dial and rotating moon dial. Five graduated nickel-plated brass tubes, signed and dated "Harris & Harrington, Patented July 30, 1901," provide the chimes at the quarter, half, three-quarters, and hour, and it strikes on the hour. A switch on the face will silence the chimes, if desired. $12,000-$15,000.

An Invitation

Hello, to each one of you who has purchased this book. Take a few minutes to come sit with me, as we visually stroll through these pages. We will feast our eyes on some items that you may never have seen before.

Matched pair of Morris reclining armchairs bearing "The Royal Chair" trademark of Sturgis, Michigan. The patented push button spring release mechanism is convenient to adjust the reclining position while in your seat. Patented May 1, l900; Called "The Push Button Kind." Right is deluxe model with footrest and bookrack. The pair were found singly within weeks of each other. Pair: $1000-$1200.

Detail: "Royal Chair" trademark.

THE
DAVIS AUTOMATIC MORRIS CHAIRS

DESIGNED FOR THOSE WHO LIKE MASSIVENESS AND SIMPLICITY OF OUTLINE, COMBINED WITH STRICTLY HIGH QUALITY OF MATERIAL, CONSTRUCTION AND FINISH. No. IK5660
EACH CHAIR FITTED WITH FOOT REST ATTACHMENT AS SHOWN IN ILLUSTRATION.

11

The Grand Entrance

Come in, we're about to go on a tour of a home absolutely filled with beautiful oak. We shall first stroll through the entry hall.

Handsome Hall Seats

Carvings at center top and backrest accentuate the beauty of the shapely beveled mirror and fancy hat hooks. $1800-$2000.

Grand in its style, this magnificent hall seat could have easily graced the lobby of a grand hotel or center hall of a prestigious home. The horseshoe-shaped beveled mirror and carved, arched crest are framed to each side by rope-twisted columns with elaborate brass hooks. Large, S-curled arms frame the boxed lift-up seat, which is contoured and carved with claw feet. Standing tall against the wall, it says, "Welcome" to all who enter. $4000-$5000.

Vibrant quartersawn grain patterns curl and swirl.

Quartersawn and stately, rope-twisted columns support the tall arms creating a deep seat. $2000-$2500.

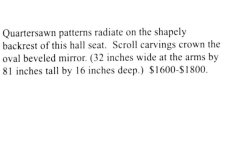

Quartersawn patterns radiate on the shapely backrest of this hall seat. Scroll carvings crown the oval beveled mirror. (32 inches wide at the arms by 81 inches tall by 16 inches deep.) $1600-$1800.

The tall rounded top is accentuated by a scroll carving curling along the edge. Quartersawn stripes are barely visible behind the darkened varnish. As shown: $1400-$1600.

Scroll carvings decorate the curved crest, back panels, and face of the storage seat. (42 inches wide by 84 inches tall by 17 inches deep.) $1500-$1800.

13

A focal point, this Pier mirror of quartersawn oak offers beauty and function with a small shelf/seat, hat hooks, and storage drawers along with its full length mirror. $1600-$1700.

A magnificent 60 inches wide; carved trumpets fanfare from the top corners above this large beveled mirror. Shaped arms with stick 'n' ball insets frame the lift-up storage seat. $4000-$5000.

A molding accentuates the top and details the mirror frame.

Never be late when you have a hall seat with a clock. Entirely of quartered oak, the pendulum clock is flanked by shaped beveled mirrors which are visually supported by large "S" curls. The boxed compartment provides a seat and storage. Shown in its darkened original varnish. $6000-$7000. A typewritten label is glued to the back stating "Directions." It tells how to level the clock and regulate the time. No manufacturer was noted.

Enormous hall seat measuring 102 inches tall by 84 inches wide by 21 inches deep from back, including its 12-inch claw feet. The years have darkened the varnish to almost black. A worn spot on the seat allows the golden quartersawn oak to shine through the years. Shown awaiting auction. Recently, sold for $8800.

A tiny postage stamp size sticker remains attached to the back. It has been facing a wall for many, many years. It reads: "TRYMBY, HUNT & CO. Manufacturers & Importers of Furniture Decorations, 1219 & 1221 Market St., Philadelphia."

Carved floral crest at center top of hall seat.

Urn-shaped columns to each side rest upon fierce lion heads overlooking scroll carved arms resembling dolphins; detail of enormous hall seat.

Unbelievable Hall Benches

Entirely of quartered oak, beautiful carvings decorate the backrest, front panel and side panels. Shaped lion head arms with claw feet are splendid. The lift-up storage seat is upholstered in leather. $2700 - $2900.

36-inch wide quartersawn hall seat with a shapely cutout back rest. An umbrella holder bracket is attached to its left side. The lift-up storage seat is handy. $1600-$1800.

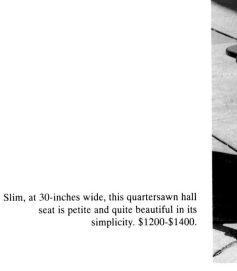

Molded top edge, claw-footed, lion-headed arm, scrolled carved back. The seat is also carved on the face and the sides.

Slim, at 30-inches wide, this quartersawn hall seat is petite and quite beautiful in its simplicity. $1200-$1400.

A center raised panel with its molded trim is set at the center backrest of this hall bench. The curled arms are supported by urn-shaped posts to each side   The face board of the boxed storage seat is a long recessed panel. The variety of raised and recessed panels give this masculine hall bench dimension. Round carved feet support the bench. Quartersawn in old darkened varnish. $1400-$1400.

Incredible carvings decorate the entire backrest and faceboard of this high quality quartered oak hall bench. Lion heads support the shaped arms then flow to the floor into claw feet.The matching hall mirror remains with this bench, but it was not available for a photograph. Quartersawn in clean darkened varnish. $2500 - $2700.

A side view of this small hall bench reveals the shapely sides with carved serpents slithering along the edge, as if slithering to reach the ground. Shown in its dusty old varnish, the quartersawn stripes still are seen across the backrest beneath the carved crest. A matching wall mirror is not shown. $1200-$1300.

Open carved, full bodied lions form the arms of this awesome hall bench designed by R. J. Horner in the late l880s; 54 inches wide by 35 inches tall, mermaids with their swirling tails and floral and leaf carvings encircle a lady's countenance. The face of the boxed lift seat is fully carved with griffins to each side. A carved crest with a lion face stands guard at the crest. $5000-$5500.

A center carved masque on the backrest of this hall bench seems serene with his eyes closed holding a slight grin. Fleur de lis carvings are set to each side. A heavy molding denotes the top above his head. The arms extend into lion heads forming the handrests. The storage seat is carved on the face with the gadrooned edge of the lid above. Big claw feet support the bench. Shown in darken, almost black, old varnish. $2000-$2500.

So cute and simple. A tiny little hall bench with its spindled back and curled arms. Scroll carving decorates the face of the storage seat.

Carved everywhere. Four vertical panels form the backrest of this elaborate carved hall bench. Each is completely filled with flower and leaf carvings, as are the two horizontal panels below on the face of the lift-seat storage chest. $2200-$2500.

Dolphins curl their tails to form the arms of this unique hall bench. The backrest is carved in two panels with a carved molding across the top. Quartersawn in its darkened old varnish. $1800-$2000.

Hall Butlers

Most unusual in its design, this hall butler seems to be holding a tray. Double shelves are supported by S-curled legs, as if to offer you something. The elliptical beveled mirror frame supports the elaborate hat hooks. Entirely of quartered oak; refinished, mirror resilvered, brass polished. $1200-$1400.

This is "Mercury" carved in quartersawn oak in mint original finish. Mercury, in Roman religion, is the god of merchandise and merchants; fleet-footed messenger of the gods. His Roman temple was dedicated in 495 BC. Artists portray him wearing winged cap and winged sandals and carrying a caduceus (staff) as you see him here. Mercury stands 83 inches tall against the wall, upon a ribbed base designed to receive umbrellas; 8-inch opening. Hooks are provided for hat and coat. He holds a 15-inch round beveled mirror. $5000-$6000, if you are lucky!

Designed to hold gloves, umbrellas, and hats, this hall butler is decorated with a variety of finely turned spindles surrounding its beveled mirror. The marble top is a nice touch with a drawer for gloves. Turned spindles are repeated on the leg supports. $1200-$1500.

Open and airy, this hall butler will hold your hat, coat, and umbrella as you enter the door, while making an interesting profile against the wall. $1200-$1400.

Hall Mirrors

The lion roars as you enter, or is he saying "Hello?" At 38 inches tall by 30 inches wide; quartersawn oak is this lion's background as he shows his full face above the oval mirrored, scroll carved, hat rack with five, double, dolphin hooks. Found in an old-time barbershop in Poughkeepsie, New York. $2200-$2400.

45 inches tall by 33 inches wide; heavily carved quartersawn with shaped beveled mirror currently sitting on the ground. $400-$450.
    Reflection: Child's rocking chair with decorative T-back. $250-$275.

Elaborate applied carvings, oval mirror. $400-$450.

    Once attached to hall seats, these carved, hat rack mirrors are now on their own to hang on the wall. These mirrors had seats similar to those on page 8 BC of *Golden Oak Furniture*.

Into the Parlor

Specifications for houses built in almost any period indicate that the space designated as the parlor or living room was to receive the best of everything—the best mantle, the finest in detailed moldings and ornamentation, the best flooring, and the hardest wall finish of any room.

The parlor has been the "traditional" room for entertaining guests so it has had to be the "best" in every respect. The need to present as good a picture to the outside world as possible has also resulted, over the years, in the continued redecoration of the room according to the dictates of fashion.

The wise old owl looks on. Standing 24 inches tall, of quartersawn oak, he watches with a keen eye and listens with a keen ear as we enter here. He perches with ivory toenails upon a book laid open upon his stand. Mint condition. Signed: J. W. Noren (origin unknown). $800-$900.

Pick Your Favorite Chair

Magnificent Morris Chairs

Open-carved griffins, to each side of a knight in armor, decorate the crest of this favorite Morris reclining armchair. Full-bodied, open-carved lions with tails curling into scrolls are on each side, forming the handrests and supporting the arms. Cabuchon posts and acanthus carved knees with claw feet support the armchair. Quartersawn, in its immaculate original varnish. $4000-$5000.

Side view of full-bodied lions and back structure without cushion.

Side view showing wings and curled tail.

Carved, winged lions, with tails wrapped around and six nicely turned spindles support the arms of this distinctive armchair. Shell carving and griffins decorate the crest. The stretcher below also is carved as it spans the distance between claw legs. $3500-$4000.

Pull Up a Footstool

Shapely, lion-headed legs stand at each corner of this footstool. $800-$900.

Incised carving decorates the sides of this Chippendale-style footstool with its ball and claw feet. The upholstered top lifts up to reveal a hideaway. $600-$700.

Regal Roman Chairs

Lion heads guard the decorated back, above its curved seat, supported by claw feet. $600-$700.

Somewhat scary, Northwind shows his angry face on the back of this Roman-style chair. Carved wings form the back, as if to protect its occupant. Shown in original finish. $400-$500.

Conservatively decorated, quartersawn oak grain shines in the sunlight on the back of this Roman-style armchair. $400-$500.

Refreshments Are Served

Tea is served, first. The tea table has beveled, glass-enclosed sides; cabriole legs have carved knees. Ball and claw feet support the cabinet, 27 inches by 18 inches by 29 inches tall. The long sides open down allowing access to the inside. The tray, 23.5 inches by 14.5 inches, lifts off if desired. $1800-$2000.

Perhaps, a dessert from this tea cart. A removable, oak-framed, glass tray with handles, can be lifted for serving. Two shelves are provided; all on rolling wheels. $500-$600.

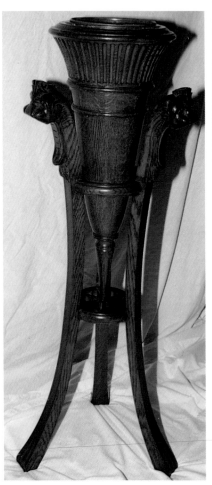

Beautiful, punch bowl stand with freestanding serpentine sides. 35 inches long by 15 inches deep at center, with a raised, circular platform to display the large crystal bowl. Scalloped railings at each end protect punch cups from falling. Carved, open-mouthed griffins with flowing manes are on guard. Shaped legs rest on a raised platform with scrolled feet. Immaculate original finish originating from a Rhode Island mansion. $2000 -$2200.

Perhaps, a little candlelight from these candles perched upon their turned oak and bronze candle holders. Pair: $600-$700.

Oh! How nice! A wine server, 37 inches tall with removable, conical, quartersawn container, and a copper insert, it rests within the tripod of the "whimsical griffin" stand in its immaculate original finish. $1600-$1800.

24

A planter in the parlor is nice. Five, heavily carved panels display well on this quartersawn planter; 30 inches wide by 10 inches deep with a tin insert to protect the wood. $800-$1000.

Set of four standing coasters hang on their rack awaiting removal to stand alone by your chair. Each is 28 inches tall to receive your glass. Set: $700-$750.

Shapely legs with stick 'n' ball stretchers add interest beneath the oval top of this tea table. $400-$450.

Detail of fireplace screen.

Incredibly beautiful fireplace screen, 46 inches tall by 28 inches wide. The center crest is a basket of open-carved flowers; carved in fine detail. Most definitely hand-carved, the floral patterns are different on each side. The tapestry is in fine condition with people on one side and animals on the other. Heavy scroll legs support this masterpiece of beauty in immaculate original finish. $8000-$9000.

Let's Make Music

This absolutely immaculate cabinet grand piano, signed Hobart M. Cable, Chicago, was found in Syracuse, New York, shortly after leaving its original owner; 63.5 inches wide by 27.5 inches deep by 56.5 inches high. Quartersawn grain dances everywhere on the cabinetry as one plays the sharp notes on the immaculate ivory keyboard. $5000-$6000.

Face panel of piano has been removed, showing the impeccably clean interior with strings and sounding board.

This is a nice view of the music cabinet's interior.

Quartersawn music cabinet of the best quality. Center meeting doors with tiny latches pivot open to reveal the music organizer interior. $1400-$1500.

Fancy Framed Mirrors

Original finish, 26 inches in diameter with incised carvings of alternating fleur-de-lis and small crests. $1200-$1300.

This heavily scroll-carved, oval mirror frame is hand-carved, without seams, from one piece of oak; 2.5 inches to 3 inches thick, 20.5 inches wide by 34 inches tall. $1500-$1600.

Currently sitting on the floor, this tall mirror wears an open-carved crest and rope-twisted columns down each side. $400-$450.

Incredibly carved with big, large fruits at its crest, this 44-inch tall by 27-inch wide oval mirror frame is stunning with its "cornucopia crest," leaf and berry carvings. $1400-$1600.

Elegantly styled, but showing its age; in very alligatored original varnish. Shaped, beveled mirror with its fancy frame and harp, fine carvings, and delicate legs give it a stylish look. $1500-$1600.

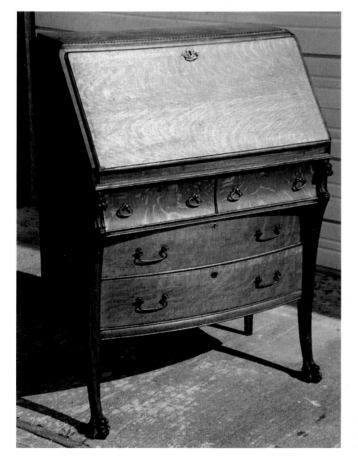

Lion heads and claw feet decorate this drop front desk with its complementing vertical concave and horizontally bowed drawer combination. $900-$1000.

Detail of desk, showing lion's head.

Carved lion heads guard the drop front of this parlor desk with its unusual rounded design and distinctive hardware. $1200-$1400.

This is another detail of the parlor desk, showing its intricate drawer front with "Northwind" drawer pulls.

This little bat, with its open mouth, accepts the key on the same desk.

A center shell carving accents this small parlor desk. $800-$900.

Incredible carvings cover this entire desk. $9000-$10,000.

A variety of curves, carving, spindles, and curls decorate this elaborate parlor desk. $1200-$1400.

More detail of the carvings of this same desk.

Winged griffins with claw feet support the corners.

Double side-by-side secretary/bookcase desk (60 inches wide) with a spindled, mirrored gallery, center drop front desk, four drawers, and two bookcases. $2400-$2800.

The entire face of this elaborate side-by-side bookcase desk is covered with beautiful scrolled carvings. $3000-$3500.

Unusual drawer pulls add to the enchantment.

A closeup shows the depth of the carved decoration.

The curved lines and shapely beveled mirror add interest to this side-by-side bookcase desk. $2500-$2800.

Elegant drop-front lady's desk with carved decoration, of excellent quality. $1500-$1600.

This is a detail view of the tall secretary desk.

The scroll carved crown and the incised carving on the drop-front desk lid accentuate this tall secretary desk perfectly. $1800-$2000.

Delicate curves of this lady's desk chair coordinate nicely with lady's desk on top right. Notice the curvature of the legs on both; they seem to belong together.

Family Room Social Time

Entertainment Armoires

An Evening at Home With the Little Ones.

Opened, grained double doors meet at center below the "wave crest."
$900-$1000.

Once a 1950s postal storage closet with two separate compartments, it has
become a most desirable entertainment center and clothing closet
combination. $1200-$1400.

Quartersawn patterns decorate the entire face of this wall cabinet. Double doors on right and a single door on left give a variety of useful spaces for entertainment items and more. $2200-$2400.

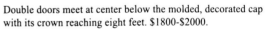

Double doors meet at center below the molded, decorated cap with its crown reaching eight feet. $1800-$2000.

Double doors meet at center post with the interior space divided. The stereo system occupies one side and the music library the other. Molded top, shaped door panels, straight grain, double drawers with contoured skirt. $1600-$1800.

Quartersawn double doors meet at center with undivided interior space. Undecorated molded top, double drawers with fancy drawer pulls. $1600-$1800.

This is a detail of the commercial suit armoire.

Straight-grained, raised panels decorate the exterior and interior of this unusual closet. Deeper than it is wide, the beveled mirrored door opens to reveal a heavy-duty pullout clothes rod and enormous drawer. Originally, a commercial suit armoire in Kraus Brothers' Men's Store, Philadelphia. $1600-$1800.

Country Closets Store "Stuff"

Undecorated, except for its wonderful grain patterns, this small armoire with shelves keeps many things put away. $900-$1000.

Interesting grain patterns travel the doors of this small closet, hinged on the inside to fold up. Label reads: K. D. Construction, Patent February 20, 1918. $900-$1000.

Long, Tall, and Short Benches

This tall, incised carved bench decorates the wall and provides special seats for guests.

All aboard! Everyone has gone to catch the train. Nine feet of bench reaches far—giving rest to many weary travelers or your holiday guests. Shown unrefinished: $500-$600.

Truly a piano bench; the back edge can be lifted and supported by a small, hinged spacer. This allows the piano player to lean into the keyboard while playing. $175-$200.

Nice saddle seat with its turned legs and many spindles. $375-$400.

Once a vanity bench, this bench received a glass top and a glass shelf laid on the stretcher below. It has become an end table. $125-$150.

Rocking Chairs of Distinction

Let's Rock on a Platform

Very heavy, signed: Hunzinger; platform rocker with upholstered back and headrest, and spindled division and lion-head finials. Big chair! Definitely a "masculine" item in immaculate original finish. $1700-$1800.

Big Hunzinger platform rocker, almost identical in design structure to the other big rocker pictured here. The only difference is the finials. Some Hunzinger rockers are dainty; these two definitely are not fragile. $1700-$1800.

Wonderful quality platform rocking chair with upholstered headrest, back, and seat. $700-$800.

Signed, "Hunzinger." This is a rare form of stick 'n' ball spindled design. Upholstered seat, back, headrest, and arms for a comfortable rock. Notice the "Y" bracket beneath the seat; a patented Hunzinger design. $1800-$1900.

Very pretty lady's platform rocker with adjustable headrest and pull-out foot rest. Known as "Mommy's Special Rocker" at home. $1000-$1200.

Very decorative platform rocking chair with turned, twisted decoration. $500-$600.

Let's Glide for a While

Detail of pressing in one of the glider rockers, shown left.

Matched pair, of high back, pressed-back, spindled, glider rockers were found separately and united within weeks of each other. Pair: $1500-$1700.

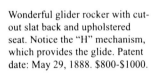

Wonderful glider rocker with cut-out slat back and upholstered seat. Notice the "H" mechanism, which provides the glide. Patent date: May 29, 1888. $800-$1000.

Arrowback glider rocker manufactured by The Wisconsin Table Company, Port Washington. Label attached. $600-$700.

Beautifully decorated and spindled fanback glider rocker. $700-$1000.

Absolutely incredible, high back, pressed-back, turned, spindled, fluted glider rocker. $900-$1200.

Put a "Spring" in Your Rock

Interesting fanback upholstered "spring rocker." The heavy coiled springs beneath support the chair and gives a "rock on air." $600-$700.

Background: A "Chautauqua desk" stands against the wall. See *Golden Oak Furniture,* page 40 TL, CTL, CTR, and page 42 TC, for more information and similar desks in the same style.

Now, Let's Rock Solid on the Floor

Advertised as a fantasy rocker, large winged swan bodies with animal feet that stand upon scaled rockers. Possibly a reclining nursing rocker? $2500-$2800.

Wonderfully elaborate, this rocker shows Northwind with a grin above the intricate spindles. The round embossed seat, triple pressings, shapely arms, turned spindles, and decorated skirt add detail. $700-$800.

High back, ladderback, quartersawn rocker with tall finials and a hand hole for easy mobility. $450-$500.

This detail, shows the skirt of the same rocker (shown above).

Triple pressings and intricate spindles decorate this rocker. $500-$600.

Tall rabbit ears and thin turned spindles make a pretty backrest chairback. $400-$500.

Elegant, comfortable, solid, sculptured seat, rocker shown in its original finish. Label reads: The Sikes Company, Philadelphia. $400-$500.

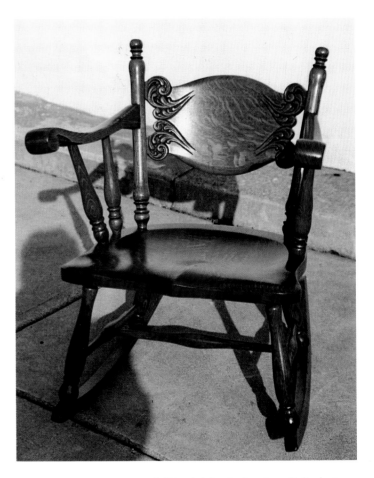

Distinctive rocker with Northwind carved back and spooled spindles. $500-$600.

Solid seated, low back rocker with its short, deeply carved backrest. $300-$400.

Solid seat and shaped center-back panel gives a comfortable rocker. $400-$450.

Beautiful empire-style rocking chair with carved accents and spindle decoration. $450-$500.

Double-pressed back rocking chair with turned side posts and bentwood arms. $500-$600.

Quartersawn, high back rocking chair with shaped triple rails for beauty and comfort. $600-$650.

Absolutely gorgeous fanback lady's rocking chair with carved crown, fancy spindles, and upholstered spring seat. $600-$700.

Very high back rocking chair with brass trim, straight slat back, and upholstered spring seat. $600-$700.

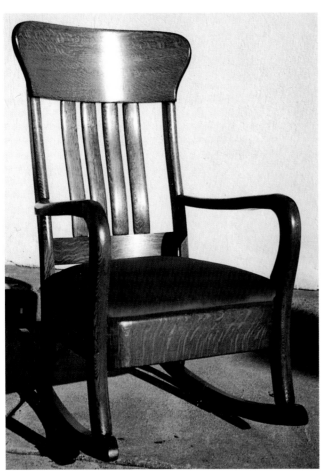

Simply comfortable rocker with contoured slat back and upholstered, spring seat. $500-$600.

In-depth, detailed pressed pattern. From decorated rocking chair, left.

Elaborately decorated solid seated rocking chair with two large
pressed panels and long, turned spindles. $600-$700.

Large pressed-back design shows off above eight long, turned spindles.
Curled bentwood arms attach to the solid seat. $600-$700.

Shapely slat back rocker awaits its upholstered seat. $400-$500.

Most elegant and comfortable in its design. $500-$600.

Large, pressed, fanback rocker with decorated back and large, turned spindles. $400-$500.

Unusual in style with its full, carved back, flat sides, and lion-head hand rests. $500-$600.

Beautiful quality, heavy duty, mission-style spring seat rocker. $700-$800.

Country ladderback rocking chair awaiting its rush seat. $200 - $300.

Intricate stick 'n' ball decorated rocking chair. $600-$700.

Pretty Parlor Tables

Oh, Those Claw Feet

This table is 24 inches square, 29 inches high with turned legs and dolphin feet. $300- $400.

Detail of dolphin in 24-inch table.

Solid quartersawn oak parlor table with square top, shaped shelf, and carved claw feet. $300-$400.

Incredible parlor table with solid quartersawn, shaped top, heavy turned legs and huge eagle talon claw and glass ball feet. $600-$800.

Parlor table with shapely top, turned legs, talon claw, and glass ball feet. $200-$300.

Left: solid quartersawn shaped top is supported by turned legs with decorative glass ball feet. Right: 24-inch square parlor table with large turned legs and huge glass ball feet. Note faces on feet. $300-$500 each.

Detail of glass ball feet, shown above.

Detail of talon claw and ball foot.

Absolutely tremendous pair of large, matching parlor tables. Shaped tops, large, heavily turned legs; huge talon claw and ball add to their style. Pair: $1200-$1400.

Spindles Galore!

Incredible, spindled table with 484 turned parts. Decorated with carved moldings, spool turnings, stick 'n' ball decorations with twisted legs. Two shelves and a drawer add convenience to the beauty of this intricate stand. $1200-$1500.

Open Rope-Twist

Tall, thin, fluted columns stand on ten-toed claw feet supporting carved "winged lions" on each corner of this 18-inch square marble topped stand. $2500-$3000.

Flowing, open rope-twisted, carved legs are beautiful supporting the round recessed top of this quality stand. Manufactured by Paine Furniture Company, Boston, Massachusetts. $800-$900.

Quartersawn beauty with four levels; carved and molded, marble top, and strong, corner legs. Shell carving shows on the base between the shapely claw-footed legs. $1600-$1800.

Quartersawn, twisted legs support the 15-inch square top of this fancy stand with its floral medallions, leaf and shell carvings decorate the apron on all sides. $1200-$1400.

Fancy urns, leaves, and scrolls with dolphins added on the front and back, are carved to decorate this strong stand. Dentil molding trims the top. $2400-$2500.

Serpentined and bombayed, this stand is 31 inches tall by 16 inches wide. No small item and most unusual. $650-$700.

Small parlor table is decorated by reverse gallery. Very decorated legs and railing on lower shelf. $250-$300.

Stick 'n' ball designs decorate the base of this rectangular parlor table, making it most desirable. $400-$500.

Graceful legs support the quartersawn top of this parlor table, decorated by its carved skirt. $300-$400.

Very substantial in design, this Eastlake-style parlor table has a large top and two shelves. $300-$400.

Beautiful in design and quality, with tapered legs, signed: The Sikes Company, Philadelphia. $300-$350.

Petite in style, this parlor table has a 14-inch top and intricately turned legs. $200-$225.

Shapely legs and decorated apron make this a pretty table. $200-$225.

Parlor table with unusually shaped, protruding legs. $200-$250.

Turned legs and shapely shelf add interest to this parlor table. $200-$225.

Quartersawn, half-moon wall table is very elegant and "French!" $400-$500.

Graceful in its lines, this shapely, half moon parlor table is beautifully decorated. $500-$600.

Elegantly oval parlor table with carved trim and reverse gallery decorating the shelf. $400-$500.

Carved, tapered legs support the round top of this parlor table. $250-$300.

Spool turned legs support the round top and shelf. Armchair and table have the same spooled turnings, but did not come together or stay together. Table: $250-$300; armchair: $350-$400.

Most unusual, this parlor table has a clover leaf design. $250-$300.

Shapely round top and shelf are supported by curved legs on this parlor table. $350-$400

Tiny six-sided parlor table with three fancy turned legs. $200-$250.

For Children to Choose a Seat

Youth size for a small derriere. Rope-twisted spindles and tall turned rabbit ears frame the pressed back. $250-$275.

This is the "cat's meow" in child's rockers. A gift to young Scarlett for her to cherish always. In darkened original finish: $350-$400.

Every child should have a parlor chair. This bow-back Sunday School style sits beside a pretty, carved lamp table with graceful, flared legs. Chair: $125-$150; table: $350-$400.

Detail of this great child's rocker, showing mother cat and kittens.

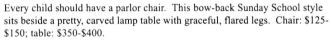

A center "lily" pressing decorates this bent-arm child's rocker. $375-$400.

Arrowback, bent-arm, solid seat child's rocker. $300-$350.

Coffee Tables

Solid quartersawn 48-inch oval with double pedestal claw-footed base. $800-$900.

Elliptical shape of vibrant quartersawn veneer; round pedestals; elongated shelf; large curled feet roll from sides. $700 - $800.

Rectangular quartersawn veneer with octagonal pedestals, shaped shelf with curled feet set on the diagonal. $600-$700.

Rectangular solid quartersawn with square pedestals. $600-$700.

Rectangular quartersawn veneer with short, turned, fluted legs and a drawer. $400-$500.

Nice 42-inch oval of quartersawn veneer with reeded columns, shaped shelf and small curled feet. $700-$800.

Collector's Cases

Originally a commercial cane display case, this glass enclosed beauty has another collection to display. The bent glass top lifts up to allow access to the inside where a grid (now acting as a shelf) is provided to support the canes and keep them separated. Small round indentations are provided on the inside bottom of the case for the end of the cane. This prevents their tips from slipping. The case is glass enclosed on all sides to allow maximum visibility of its contents. If you look closely, the ripples of the old glass are caught in the light and resemble radiating heat. $2000-$2500.

Dental supply cabinet of quartersawn oak. Sectional units consist of base, three chests with seven levels of drawers in each and the cap. Many shallow drawers currently house an extensive jewelry collection. The label holders with finger pulls are polished brass; original to the cabinet. Perfect refinished condition. $1200-$1500.

Dental instrument cabinet (36 inches wide by 16 inches deep by 46 1/2 inches to top plus 6 inches mirror back) of solid quartersawn oak radiates its grain patterns. A narrow mirror stands above the marble work surface. A variety of small drawers and compartments are provided. These visually are separated from the larger drawers and cabinet below by squared columns. These continue to the floor into the legs, wearing brass cuffs standing on original 2-inch ball-bearing castors. The sides are deeply set recessed panels showing vibrant graining. $2000-$2500.

Cabinets to Hide Away Things

The painted floral panels of this cabinet were preserved and reset into their oak frames. Of quartersawn oak, the cabinet was all black; panels were removed to refinish the cabinet. 54 inches across the back with diagonal side panels. $1800-$2000.

Quartersawn, pedestal table with two drawers and handy drop sides. $900-$1000.

Stunning music cabinet decorated with intricate brass trimmings. Currently, resides in a breakfast area. $900-$1000.

This view shows the inside compartment of the humidor.

Humidor smoking stand, door opens to reveal a porcelain lined, air-tight compartment for tobacco products. $450-$500.

Actually, a quartersawn child's sideboard. Dimensions of 25 inches wide by 16 inches deep by 18 inches tall, plus the 12-inch mirrored back, makes it ideal for an end table with display and storage. $750-$800.

Really nice lift-top storage chest, pressed patterns cover the drawer faces and sides of this cabinet. $800-$1000.

Detail of lift-top storage chest.

Seven shallow drawers are great for papers of any kind.

Beautiful, quality quartersawn oak, this small stand has a round convertible top. It can be round or half-round to stand against the wall with its half up or down. $800-$1000.

Very unique, small cabinet with six mini-drawers and medicine chest type compartment behind its beveled mirrored door. $900-$1000.

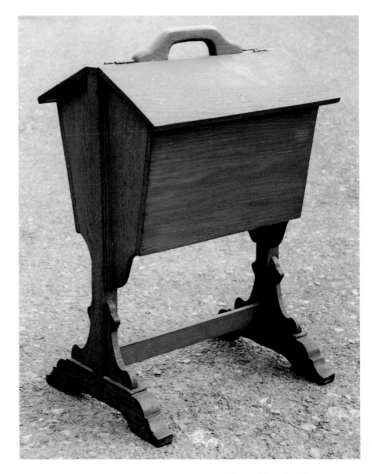

Quartersawn grain and shapely legs are graceful on this music cabinet, now lamp table. The front drops forward allowing access to storage. $450-$500.

Unusual in oak, this knitting stand has double lift tops with storage. $275-$300.

Incised carvings decorate the sides and fancy board of this Eastlake-style music stand. $450-$500.

Accents Everywhere!

Jardiniere Stands and Taboret Tables

S-curls, at each corner, follow the vertical serpentine lines of this squatty 15-inch square-topped, 20-inch high stand. A handle is provided to permit easy moving. The pair, in front of a sofa, are most handy when outfitted with glass tops; nubbins provided. Immaculate original condition. Pair: $1500-$1600.

Serpentine sides and shapely legs of this 16 inches square by 19 inches high stand are most eye-catching. Quartersawn veneer in original finish. $500-$600.

S-curled lions with "goatees" support this 15 inches high by 18.5 inches in diameter stand with its double-ringed, quartersawn, one piece top. $750-$800.

Six bombayed sides meet at a point on this 16.5 inches by 20 inches high stand, supported by three lion-headed, claw-footed legs. Quartersawn veneer in original finish. $750-$800.

Six-sides, with beaded trim "in spades." $150-$175.

Darker in color, claw-footed lions balance the 17 inches in diameter, quartersawn, top of this 19-inch high stand. Signed: Grand Rapids Manufacturing Co., Seal of Quality. $750-$800.

Stick 'n' ball design. Quite collectible. $200 - $250.

Six sides; solid quartersawn with intricately pressed pattern sides. $250-$300.

Quartersawn round with scalloped top. Shapely, cutout sawtooth legs.
$250-$275.

Solid quartersawn; square top with turned legs and boxed base. In a rich
darkened varnish. $300-$350.

Square top; four panels cutout at center to form legs. $250-$275.

Undecorated except for its cutout pattern.
$130-$150.

71

Boxed top is decorated with stick 'n' ball patterns. $200-$250.

Intricate bentwood, stick 'n' ball stand. $250-$300.

Curly legs support the two
shelves. $275-$300.

Pretty pedestal stand with scalloped 14-inch round top, shaped pedestal and decorated platform base; 17 inches tall. $275-$325.

Ball and claw foot parlor table in miniature; a salesman's sample. $275-$300.

Rope-twisted tapered pedestal stand. $275-$300.

Distinctive chair-side stand with incised carved apron, cabriole legs with claw feet. $275-$300.

Incredible Pedestals

Muscled and fierce, this griffin is a full 12 inches wide and 12 inches deep. In his crouching position with wings back, he balances the round top upon his head as he sits on the rectangular base with bun feet. Of quartersawn oak, carved in detail, with a furrowed brow and hairy chest. Incredible! $4500-$5500.

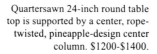

Quartersawn 24-inch round table top is supported by a center, rope-twisted, pineapple-design center column. $1200-$1400.

Nice guy! This 36-inch tall muscled young man stands, in his loin cloth, with his arms crossed and one foot forward. He supports the round top with his curly haired head, while standing on his round platform. Quartersawn oak. $1700-$1900.

Rear view showing muscled legs, back, and details of wings.

A graceful, carved, 12 inches tall by 4 inches thick dolphin decorates this 39-inch tall pedestal stand, as he supports the 16-inch by 20-inch top with his opened carved tail. $3800 - $4000.

Tall 42-inch twin pedestals, with 8.5-inch pineapple design; turned, tapered, fluted columns with shaped top; platform base with scaled, claw feet. Pair: $1300-$1400.

A 36-inch tall whimsical lion with his mouth open looks on as he supports the round top of this 44-inch tall pedestal stand. $900-$1000.

Four, large, paw feet support the thick, rope-twisted column with its square top and small skirt. $800 -$850.

To light your way, a pair of 45-inch tall, fluted pedestal, candle stands with acanthus carvings below the shaped top supporting the turned candle holders. The column rests on a round, turned base with three carved claw feet. Pair: $1200-$1300.

75

Small and "meaty"; 30 inches tall with heavy, 1.5 inches thick, carved C-scrolls wrapping around the bulbous 10-inch diameter middle, tapering to 8 inches, resting on a heavy scrolled footed base. A marble top with clipped corners sits above the carved border. Quite unusual in its shape. $1800-$2000.

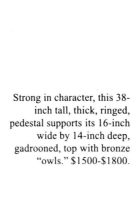

Strong in character, this 38-inch tall, thick, ringed, pedestal supports its 16-inch wide by 14-inch deep, gadrooned, top with bronze "owls." $1500-$1800.

This table is 33 inches tall with triple, 3-inch square columns standing on a rounded, claw-footed platform supporting the 16-inch diameter, quartersawn, top. $700-$800.

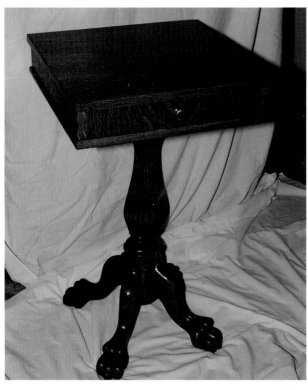

The square table top with its small drawer is supported by a tapered, fluted pedestal with four carved, claw-footed legs. $650-$700.

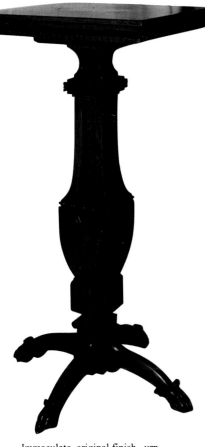

"Tallyho!" There's the fox, mounted on oak. Fox-hunting scenes are displayed in their oak frame. Fox in perfect condition: $200-$250; picture: $250-$275.

Wall Furniture

Immaculate, original finish, urn-shaped, carved pedestal with its square, molded, top and claw-footed legs stands squarely on the floor. $1500-$1600.

This 43-inch tall, muscled, carved, quartersawn man holds his round, 14.5-inch diameter top with one hand and his garment with the other, as he stands on his claw-footed platform. $1800-$2000.

Flat wall, locking, curio cabinet. Fox-hunting collectibles are easily viewed in wallhanging curio cabinets. This cabinet and the two following are good examples. $275-$300.

A cast iron, oak trimmed, bridle holder once resided in a stable. It is currently a great doorstop. It sits upon a small stool with lift-up top. Holder: $75-$100; stool: $75-$85.

Small corner, locking curio cabinet. $275-$300.

There's the horse! He's watchful with ears tucked back. The molded metal form is mounted on an oak backing set within a nickel-plated copper horseshoe. 24-inch tall and meant to be mounted on a wall. $250 - $300.

Flat wall curio with double-beaded board back. Paint on the outside was removed, but remains on the inside to give a "rustic look." $250-$275.

Raised-panel, quartersawn corner cabinet with its spindled gallery. $750-$850.

Tiny, brass beads decorate the beveled sides and face of this corner medicine cabinet with its scrolled crest. $350-$400.

Multiple mirrors dazzle the face of the 36-inch tall by 20-inch wide medicine cabinet. Decorated by its tall open-carved crest with detailed molding all around top and bottom and raised panel quartersawn sides. $1400-$1600.

Cute hanging medicine chest with beveled mirror. $250.

Country-style with double glass doors. $250-$300.

Bentwood, spindled wall pocket with musical lyre design. $150-$175.

A round mirror in its square frame with triangular corner blocks, decorated with incised "butterprint" flowers and leaf pattern. $275-$300.

Once a parlor organ top, it has become a most prized curio shelf. $500-$600.

Incised Eastlake-style carvings decorate this curio shelf, which was once a top to a parlor icebox. 38 inches tall by 35 inches wide by 7 inches deep. $400-$450.

Dinner Is Served in the Dining Room

Comfortable Upholstered Seating

Detail of Belter laminated oak side chair. Rear view showing the shape of the back.

One of an incredible set of seven elaborately carved formal dining chairs. The cabochon center crest rises high above the carved ladies to each side of the serpentine chair back and seat. An inverted crest decorates the lower rail between the shapely acanthus carved paw feet. These sets were originally sold in good, better, and best. In immaculate condition of the best grade. Set of seven: $11,000-$12,000.

Classic example of John Henry Belter (1850-1860) laminated oak side chair, a rare form of his work. As a single: $2400-$2500.

The fancy chair to the left shows carved masques on its crest and finials. Right: Floral carved crest, twisted spindles, rungs, and legs. These two chairs were united into a collection of similar chairs to accommodate the dining room. Left: $500-$600; right:$400-$500.

This closeup shows the carved mask of the fancy upholstered chair above.

This carved armchair resides in a foyer; matching side chair in a fancy dining room.

Elegant, quartersawn, T-back style; graceful lines, vibrant grain patterns with a center accentuating carving. Floral fabric replaced original leather seats. Label reads "Grand Rapids, Michigan." Set of six: $2000-$2200.

Quartersawn T-back style; curved back panel and shapely legs with tiny claw feet. Set of six including two armchairs: $1800-$2000.

Center: single, quartersawn, T-back style dining chair with flowing lines and cutout center back panel united with a set of five to even the set. As a single: $150-$200. Left and right: Beautifully shaped and cut out center back panel; shaped legs with ankles and large claw-feet. Set of five, including one armchair: $1800-$2000.

Quartersawn T-back style with delicate accent carving above the pierced backs. Shown awaiting its upholstered spring seats. Set of five: $1800-$2000.

Quartersawn T-back style with center cabochon carving. Cabriole legs with ribbing has interest. Set of six, including two armchairs: $2000-$2200.

Quartersawn pierced T-back style. Boxed upholstered seat and great claw feet. Set of four: $900-$1000.

Tightly grained, quartersawn T-back style with undecorated pierced-back panel. Shaped boxed seat; graceful legs with ankles and "almost claw feet." Set of four: $900-$1000.

Elegant Queen Anne style dining chairs. Two side chairs and one armchair remain from the original set. The flowing lines and shapely curves are beautiful. Shapely legs stand on large carved claw feet. Pair of side chairs: $700-$800; armchair: $700-$800.

Matching quartersawn armchairs with double vertical, decorated back panels. Tapered legs with ankles and big claw feet. Pair: $800-$900.

Exceptional quartersawn with carved crest, many finely turned spindles, upholstered backrest and seats. Thirty-nine inches tall, this elegant chair stands on shapely legs. Set of seven: $2800-$3200.

Stately quartersawn armchairs with comfortable rounded arms and upholstered leather seats. Pair: $1200-$1400.

Delightful Dining in Handsome Chairs

Tall, quartersawn, double-pressed, fanback dining chair with turned one piece back leg construction, caned seat, skirt, three turned rungs. As a pair: $500-$600.

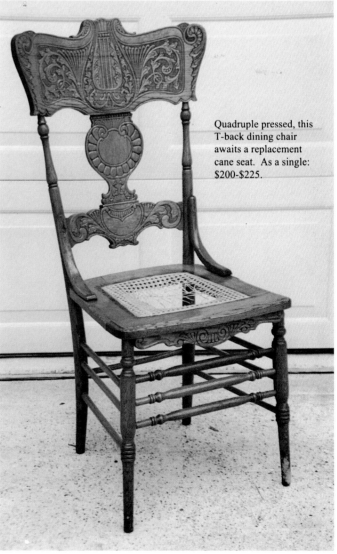

Quadruple pressed, this T-back dining chair awaits a replacement cane seat. As a single: $200-$225.

Triple pressings decorate this tall fanback dining chair. Notice the exceptional skirt below the caned seat. Set of four: $1200- $1400.

Double pressed with intricate patterns of sunflowers. $1600-$1800.

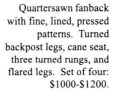

Detail of dining chair with sunflower pressed pattern.

Quartersawn fanback with fine, lined, pressed patterns. Turned backpost legs, cane seat, three turned rungs, and flared legs. Set of four: $1000-$1200.

Double pressed fanback dining chair with flowing scroll pressings, turned backpost legs with three rungs, and reeded front legs; small skirt. Set of four: $1200-$1500.

Tall "smiling" set of six double pressed-back dining chairs with turned sideposts, twisted spindles, embossed leather seats, turned legs, three turned rungs, flared legs, and a small skirt. Set of six: $1600-$1800. Detail below.

Double pressed with rabbit ears, spindles, cane seat, small skirt, triple turned rungs, and flared legs. Coordinated well with a 42-inch round claw-foot pedestal table. Set of four: $1000-$1200.

Double pressed with beaded cameo pattern; spindles and caned seat. Legs are turned joined by three rungs. Pair: $450-$500.

Dazzling in its height, triple pressed, tall pressed-back dining chair. The space between the top and second rails provides a handgrip to pull the chair away from the table. Flared legs, with turnings resembling anklets. Set of four: $1500-$1700.

Double pressed with rabbit ears, spindles, and cane seat. Set of five: $1100-$1200.

Tall fluted rabbit ears, spindles, cane seat; press on skirt. Set of three: $500-$600.

Triple pressed with tall turned rabbit ears, spindles, turned single post back legs, cane seat, and nice skirt. Set of six: $1600-$1800.

Pressed T-back dining chair with its decorated headpiece and shaped center back panel. Set of four: $1200-$1400.

Bentwood spindles of this double pressed fanback dining chair take your eye to the center cameo pattern. Reeded backpost legs, caned seat, and small skirt. Set of four: $1200-$1400.

This chair shows a single press above plain tapered spindles. The unusual seat appears solid, but it is not. A square center panel is dovetailed into the outside framework of the seat allowing expansion of the seat with the weight of its occupant. Three rungs front and side with two in the rear give the chair strength. Set of six: $1600-$1800.

This is a closeup view of the dovetailed square center panel seat.

Quartersawn grain patterns show on the cameo pressed pattern of this dining chair.
As a single: $200-$300.

Chairs appear to be the same from a distance, however, they are not. The spindles bend the same, but have different turnings. The embossed design on the headpieces are complementary, but not the same. The outline is slightly different. This pair invokes special interest as well as being beautiful. Pair: $500-$600.

Pressed-back chair on right; detail of photo, left.

Pressed-back chair on left; detail of photo, above.

The scrolled pressing stands tall above the spindles and the "dished" solid seat. The dip in the seat provides better comfort for the body while sitting. Turned legs, turned rungs, and flared legs had style. Set of six: $2000-$2200.

Two similar pairs of chairs joined to make an interesting set of four. Both have wide fanbacks and similar lines of design.
Left: Double pressed with floral pressed fanback, caned seat with embossed skirt. Pair: $400-$500. Right: Double pressed with embossed fanback, caned seat with scalloped skirt. As a pair: $400-$500.

Tall fluted rabbit ears, single pressing, spindles, woven cane seat without skirt. Notice the two diagonal rungs beneath the seat adding strength to the chair. Slightly flared legs. As a single: $150-$200.

The quartersawn horizontal rails forming the back are curved and decorated and most comfortable. The boxed caned seat is contoured. The legs have a flowing line to the floor. Set of four: $ 1200-$1500.

Detail of ladderback dining chair.

Single ladderback-style dining chair with a beautiful, decorated, deeply embossed, head rail. Notice the visual depth of the design enhanced by the stippled background of the pressed pattern. Turned single post back legs support the chair. As a single: $175-$200.

Quartersawn ladderback dining chair with caned seat and shapely legs. One of two side chairs and two armchairs in this set. Set: $1400-$1600.

Swirling pressed patterns decorate triple pressed, spindled, well made dining chair. Set of four: $1400-$1500.

The shapely outline of this quartersawn dining chair gives it a beautiful look of quality, which it is. Set of four: $1000-$1200.

Open oak graining shows on the back of this solid seated dining chair. The round seat and softened lines of the back give this set of four a nice look. Set: $1000-$1200.

Single pressed-back dining chair with a T-back construction. The headpiece is carved, giving depth to the design. Nice decorative chair for use anywhere. $150-$175.

Pressed T-back with decorative center panel. Shaped seat and tapered legs. Pair: $400-$500.

Basic set of six solid seated dining chairs. Not fancy, but serviceable and durable. Set: $800-$1000.

Nice quality set with center upholstered back, decorated above and below by scroll carvings. The boxed seat is caned. The legs taper to the floor with ankles. Set of six: $1800-$2000.

A set of six smaller pressed-back chairs were united with this similar set of five, on each side, to make a very nice set of eleven complementing dining chairs to serve a large family. Both sets share the same pressed-back pattern, turned spindles and solid seats. It is unusual to find such a match. Shown here are three chairs of the set. Two sizes in chairs of similar design were often offered by the same manufacturer. Set of six: $1600-$1800.

Turned rabbit ears stand above the embossed head rail. The side posts are braced by "hiphuggers," where they join the solid seat. Legs and double rungs are turned. Originally for dining, this set is currently in the waiting room as seating in a physician's office. Chosen for durability. Set of six: $1500-$1800.

Detail of pressed head rail of same chair.

Tall turned rabbit ears and turned side posts frame the pressed headrail and the spindles of this pretty chair. Hiphuggers give the back reinforcement. Set of five: $1400-$1600.

Wonderful solid seated pressed-back dining chair with its tall, wide, embossed back and long turned spindles and contoured seat. Set of four: $1200-$1500.

Vibrant quartersawn graining displayed on the back of this chair is created by the use of specific veneers. The round seat supported by tapered legs adds elegance to this set of chairs. Set of four: $1200-$1400.

Pressed-back, spindled, solid seated kitchen chairs found their home with a drop leaf extension table for a great country-style kitchen look. Set of six: $1200-$1400.

Small scale pressed-back set of six dining chairs. Turned rabbit ears frame the center pressing with spindles connecting the lower pressed rail. Light weight in structure and appearance. Set: $750 - $850.

The fanback is of ply construction with a decorated handgrip and pierced center panel. Several thicknesses of wood are bonded together to form this back. Quartersawn veneer is then applied to the chair to produce the radiating grain patterns. The seat is contoured to fit the body and is also veneered to match the back. The legs are turned just under the seat and flair to the floor. Three turned rungs give strength and detailing to the chair's design. Set of four: $1200 - $1400.

This is another detail of the fanback chair of 5-ply construction.

Five plys can be seen if one looks closely.

One armchair and three side chairs make up this set of quartersawn dining chairs. The top line is a nice wave. The center panel is detailed with scrolling to accentuate the shapely outline of the center back panel. The legs flow gracefully to the floor. Set: $800- $1000.

Combining rattan into this design is most unusual. Notice the different style of chair braces on this chair. The seat is leather, supported by heavy turned legs with thick turned rungs. Notice the angle of the rear legs as they project backward. This inhibits the occupant from trying to rock in a dining chair. If they do, the strength of the leg is at the vertical line so it will not break. Set of four: $1200-$1500.

Center: One of two quartersawn dining chairs with tall fanback, shaped, pierced center back panel and boxed seat. Caned seats were replaced by upholstery for a more elegant look. As a pair: $500-$600. Left and right: Set of four quartersawn T-back dining chairs. Undecorated, but showing beautiful grain patterns across the backs. The caned, boxed seat has a nice scallop across the front and shapely legs with carved claw feet. $1100-1200. These four and two were united to make a complementary set.

Very basic solid seated T-back dining chair with shaped panel back. Set of four; $400-$600.

Basic quartersawn T-back dining chair has nice lines; vibrant graining, caned, boxed seat with shaped legs. Set of four: $600-$700.

This single armchair shows the shapely outline of its pierced center panel. An upholstered seat has replaced the cane seat. The shaped arms are rolled on the ends to accommodate the palms comfortably. The legs have a nice contour to the floor. This is a nice extra chair, or add it to a set. As a single: $250-$300.

Plain, but stylish pair of T-back dining chairs. Nice lines, cane seats and flared legs add to their style. Pair: $350-$400.

Graceful T-back armchair with shapely center panel, upholstered seat, and nice shapely legs. As a single: $200-$250.

Fancy pressed-back armchair with tall rabbit ears, double pressings, bentwood arms, spindles, and caned seat. As a single: $500-$600.

Basic upholstered T-back armchair with straight legs. As a single: $150-$175.

Two of six tiny pressed-back child's chairs have a matching pedestal dining table of their own (not shown). This set was a gift at birth to Cara Marie, now six, from Aunt Fran, one of the last Victorian ladies. Set of six, chairs only: $600-$700.

Signed and validated by certificate from the Heywood Wakefield Company, this set of arrowback, pressed-back chairs are very nice. Set of four: $1200-$1400.

Detail of child's chair.

Holiday Dining Tables Can Be Every Day's Pleasure

Unusually designed 42-inch round dining table. Sets of scrolled legs with claw feet hug the center pedestal when closed. Upon opening, legs move outward providing stability for the extended table. $1800-$2000.

45-inch round dining table with two leaves; straight grained top, large fluted pedestal with large knuckled claw feet. $1800-$2000.

45-inch round dining table; turned, fluted pedestal with carved heads standing above the carved claw feet. $1800-$2000.

42-inch round dining table with a straight grained top. The pedestal is tapered and fluted from top to bottom. The legs extend from the pedestal, with a low slope, into nicely carved claw feet. $1600-$1800.

Dining table is 47 inches round, with six cabriole legs, quartersawn veneer top and two 8-inch solid extension leaves. Graceful looking. Labels attached read: "For Hecht Bros. Co.; 681 W. Baltimore St. Maryland from Sterling Furniture Co.,Greensboro, N.C. $600-$700.

42-inch round dining table with solid quartersawn top and three original leaves. The pedestal is turned with four rings accentuating the curl of the legs as they meet the pedestal. The legs gracefully slope and curl to the floor. $1000-$1200.

Pressed-back chairs: Set of four are actually two similar pairs mated to make a set. The pressing match each other, two chairs have spindled backs and two chairs have a center panel back. Nice set. Set of four: $800-$1000.

48-inch round, solid quartersawn dining table with its six-sided pedestal and wide, sloping, square cut legs resting on square pad feet. Two quartersawn leaves. A very substantial table. $1200-$1400.

Beautiful 42-inch solid quartersawn pedestal dining table with claw feet. Notice the beautiful graining of the top with its beveled edge and the contoured apron beneath. This table shows the quality and the "look" of tables made by the Hastings Table Company, Hastings, Michigan. Two quartersawn leaves. $1400-$1600.

42-inch round pedestal dining table with a nice straight grained top and three grain matched extension leaves. The pedestal is nicely turned above the high rounded knees as they join the pedestal and then slope into carved claw feet. $1500-$1700.

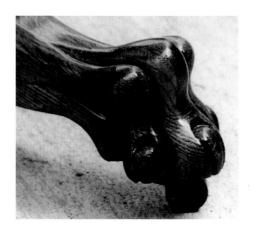

This detail shows the desirable style of the claw foot with three high knuckles and carved toenails.

48-inch round solid quartersawn claw-foot pedestal dining table. The pedestal is plain without turnings, but the decoration is on the legs as they meet the pedestal. Notice the contour on the edge of the leg as it flows into the claw foot giving a graceful line to the leg. $1600-$1800.

107

45-inch round solid quartersawn dining table dressed up with its beaded apron. Five large, fancy, tapered, turned, fluted legs support the table which extends to accommodate its three leaves. $1200-$1400.
Background: The quartersawn mirror hanging on the wall is quite interesting as it displays a very curvy beveled mirror. $250-$300.

This is a closeup of two of the five legs of the 45-inch round dining table.

The pedestal on this beautiful 54-inch round solid quartersawn, split pedestal dining table divides at center to support the table when it is extended with its three quartersawn leaves. Large rope-twisted columns decorate the otherwise straight lines of the pedestal. The label attached reads: "Hastings Table Company, Hastings, Michigan." Awaiting pickup after restoration. A real beauty. $3000-$3500.

This claw foot pedestal dining table base supports a 42-inch round straight grained top that accommodates four grain matched leaves. The pedestal shows straight grain on its barrel and on its legs. Notice the square cut to the leg itself. The claw foot design is nice, with three knuckles and carved "spurs." $1200-$1400.

Split pedestal base supports a 48-inch round solid quartersawn dining table top. The pedestal is constructed of two halves which latch together when extension is not needed. The legs are carved, sloping into knuckled claw feet. These knuckles are of equal heights giving more of a flattened claw. $2000-$2200.

48-inch round, solid quartersawn, claw-footed pedestal dining table of quality, having high kneed claw-footed legs; large knuckles and toenails. Selected lumber created the grain patterns. Three leaves extend the table. $1600-$1800.

This heavily carved pedestal with its incredible, large, carved claw feet supports the 54-inch round solid quartersawn top of this beautiful dining table. Attached label reads: "Hastings Table Company, Hastings, Michigan." Notice the contoured apron, which is a characteristic feature of tables attributed to this company. Part of the original furnishings of an affluent 1909, Long Beach Island, New Jersey shore home, this table was retrieved with a set of dining chairs; both had seen much neglect. This table now sits in a bright eating area overlooking a pool, at home near the water. $3000-$3500.

45-inch round, close grained, solid quartersawn pedestal dining table with an elegantly tapered fluted pedestal. The shaped legs have high knees and great carved claw feet. $1600-$1800.

A close-up view shows one claw foot of the 45-inch round table with the fluted pedestal.

Solid quartersawn patterns are visible on the top of this 42-inch round pedestal dining table. The edge of the table is rounded and the apron is straight as is the pedestal. The knees are "feathered" with sloping legs ending in narrow claw feet, which are no wider than the leg. Each toe has a large carved toenail. Label reads: "Penn Furniture Company, Philadelphia, Pa." $1500-$1600.

Elegant 42-inch square solid quartersawn extension dining table with shell decorated shaped apron; turned, tapered, fluted with unusual elongated claw feet.

Detail view of legs of 42-inch square dining table.

Enormous turned, tapered, fluted legs support this straight grained 44-inch square extension table. The table apron is tapered inward, directing your eye to the legs. With six original leaves. $2200-$2500.

Solid quartersawn rectangular dining table (42 inches by 46 inches) with eight decoratively turned legs and nine 8 inch original grain matched extension leaves. The corner legs are attached by stretchers to a third leg in a "V" shape. When not extended, the four legs at center nest together. When extended, the outside three move away from the two middle legs giving distributed support to the table as needed. $2300-$2500.

United with a beautiful set of upholstered dining chairs, the combination made a nice looking and very versatile dining set. Notice how the "clipped" corners on the table add character.

Four decorative claw-footed legs and double center legs support the 45-inch square top of this dining room table. $1000-$1200.

Five graceful turned, tapered, and fluted legs support the top of this 44-inch quartersawn dining table. The apron is grooved, which adds a nice look. With three leaves. $1400-$1600.

Six very decoratively turned and shaped legs support this 45-inch square dining table. Notice the bow of the apron and the carved stretcher. $1500-$1800.

Rectangular dining table, 42 inches by 32 inches, with five square, turned legs; opens with three leaves. $1200-$1400.

Heavy, twisted, claw-footed legs support the quartersawn top of this 45-inch square dining table with two 12-inch leaves. $1800-$2000.

36-inch square table, extends on each end by pullout leaves stored under the table top. $500-$600.

Fancy turned legs with their decorated center panel support this quartersawn table top. Notice the similarity between the table legs and the chair legs. Even though they did not originate together, they make a nice set. Table, $1200; set of four chairs, $800.

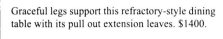

Graceful legs support this refractory-style dining table with its pull out extension leaves. $1400.

Five decorated claw-footed legs support this 42-inch square quartersawn table top. Notice the tapering of the apron. $1200-$1400.

The scroll carved apron is unusual. A 48-inch square solid quartersawn top is supported by shaped legs with carved stretcher panel. $1500 - $1800.

Sideboards to Serve

Nicely carved, this crystal cabinet sideboard shows its bowed glass enclosed curio, shaped mirrors, carvings, and turnings beautifully, and it provides display and storage space. $5500-$6500.

S-curls support the shelves of this stunning sideboard. Heavily carved crest with overlooking carved masque. $2000.

Detail of sideboard with close view of crest with carved masque.

Wonderful carved sideboard with bowed, glass enclosed curio cabinet and triple mirrors. $6000-$6500.

Oval beveled mirror; shapely shelf supports carved trim and detailing creates an elegant look to this sideboard. $1800-$2000.

Shaped beveled mirror, carved columns, carved crest and decorated doors. $2000-$2200.

Winged lion from massive sideboard.

Massive, heavily carved sideboard with five beveled mirrors, deep canopy top with a carved "jester" looking out. Full carved, winged lions support the shelves which house secret drawers. The silver and linen drawers are cylindrical, the base cabinet doors bow vertically to meet the carved lion face at center. Claw feet support this most admired item. $3500-$4000.

Carved lion face, same sideboard.

Jester from the same sideboard.

Shapely and beautiful, this sideboard is enhanced by its beveled mirror and shapely shelf supports. $1800-$2000.

The tall carved crest of this sideboard makes a crown enhancing the softened lines of the curved drawers. $1800-$2000.

Stunning, with two full width shaped mirrors divided by a horizontal shelf supported by rope-twisted columns. Serpentine drawers and carved doors are framed by the rope-twisted corner posts. $4500-$4700.

Foreground: 60-inch round pedestal table. See *Golden Oak Furniture,* back cover and page 51, BL.

Detail, showing closeup
view of massive sideboard.

Striking, heavily carved, massive sideboard shows many carvings, twists,
turnings and, best of all, the jester guarding its domain. $5000-$6000.

Detail, showing jester.

Beautiful Buffets and Servers

Absolutely gorgeous 66-inch wide buffet sideboard, with carved column corners, carved doors and drawers, supported by four large claw feet. Exceptional drawer pulls with interesting faces. $4000- $4500.

This is a good view of one of the wonderful drawer pulls on the 66-inch wide buffet.

On the left, a small scale quartersawn buffet shows clean lines without decoration other than its graining. At 36-inches tall, it is perfect serving height, and its 54-inch width fills the wall space. The 13-inch mirrored back offers a 3-inch shelf. The top drawer appears to be divided, but it is one full width drawer for the linens. Two center drawers and two compartments offer additional storage. Tall square legs support this buffet. Maker's label reads: "Made by J. K. Rishel Furniture, Williamsport, PA." $1200-$1400.
Right: See China Cabinets, page 126.

Empire style sideboard shows its vibrant quartersawn grain pattern, nice S-curls, short mirror supporting a small curio shelf. $1000-$1200.

Massive buffet is heavily decorated with its carved back, huge fancy brass drawer pulls and unique shape to its lower double doors. $2000-$2200.

Nicely styled buffet with fluted columns, decorative carvings, barrel drawers, and vibrant quartersawn grain. $1000-$1200.

Very pretty server buffet with bowed glass, curio cases on each side of the drawer and/or storage. Serving surfaces enhanced by its shaped beveled mirrored back. $1600-$1700.

Solid quartersawn mission-style buffet. Desirable size and style; angular, long and shallow. $1600-$1800.

Beautiful, heavy, fancy brass pulls decorate the doors above unusually carved double door storage compartment. $900-$1000.

Elegant in its look, quartersawn stripes shine on the face of this server. The shapely beveled mirrored back enhances the crystal collection. $1500-$1700.

Beautifully decorated, this server shows its carved splashboard, carved drawer and double shelves supported by lion heads. $900-$1000.

Detail of server, showing carved splashboard and a lion head.

So very plain, this tiny side server fits perfectly on a small wall to provide a display area and storage. $500.

Charming China and Curio Cabinets

Beautiful, quartersawn, rope-twisted china closet is 54-inches across the back with bowed sides. $3800-$4000.

Quartersawn corner cabinet with triple flame finials at its crest with a beveled glass enclosed display area, drawer, and raised panel cabinet doors. $6000-$6500.

Delicate carvings and tiny beads outline the molded top.

Front and rear; scaled and detailed claw feet.

Elegant china and/or curio display cabinet with center double bowed doors and shaped glass enclosed cabinets to each side. Shapely triple mirrors decorate the gallery. $8000-$9000.

The graceful, scroll-carved crest stands tall above the bowed enclosure of this china closet and its treasures. $2000-$2200.

Vibrant graining radiates on the quartersawn frame of this china/curio cabinet. The glass shelves and mirrored back shine clearly through the outside glass showing the waves of age. $1200-$1400.

Stunning bowed glass china closet with carved canopy top, supporting columns with capitals resting on the platform base with its giant claw feet. It appears to be a glass bubble inside its framework. $5000-$5500.

Outstanding corner china closet with center leaded glass panel, framed to each side by bowed glass doors enclosing its mirror backed display area. The gallery is guarded by its center griffin supporting the curio shelf. Its overall height is 75 inches to center crest; 21 inches deep at each side. $3800-$4000.

Detail of china closet shows griffin supporting the curio shelf.

Beautiful bowed glass sides with carved crest above the center door with its drawer and claw-footed base. $4000-$4500.

This view shows the bow of the glass and the carved canopy of the china closet.

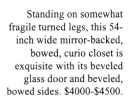

Standing on somewhat fragile turned legs, this 54-inch wide mirror-backed, bowed, curio closet is exquisite with its beveled glass door and beveled, bowed sides. $4000-$4500.

Very nice bowed glass china closet stands on its tiny carved claw feet, basically undecorated but pretty in its simplicity. $1200-$1500.

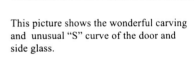

Elegant, quartersawn serpentined glass enclosed china closet. Notice the "S" curvature of the door and side glass. Details of carvings add to its beauty. $3200-$3500.

This picture shows the wonderful carving and unusual "S" curve of the door and side glass.

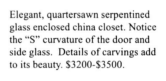

Stunning 54-inch wide, mirror-back china closet with tall arched and molded crest, serpentine glass sides and bowed door flanked by large turned columns and carving; all standing on large five-toed claw feet. $5500-$6000.

Quartersawn mission-style china closet with two mirrored shelves. Currently house a Civil War memorabilia collection. Label attached to back reads: "K. C. Co., Chester, PA." $1400-$1500.

More bowed than most, this quartersawn china closet is tall with its five levels of display standing on carved claw feet. $1800-$2000.

A mirrored gallery rests on the top of this bowed glass china closet. Carved columns accentuate the rounded door. Claw feet support the case. $1800-$2000.

A good look at one of the lion heads on the mirrored top of the same china cabinet.

Quartersawn china cabinet with lion-head mirrored top. Carved and fluted columns frame the bowed door above carved claw feet. Sticker reads: "Ship to Julia A. Borgeson, Glenmore, PA." $1800-$2000.

Serpentined side glass curves forward to meet the vertical columns framing the serpentined center door. Quartersawn graining shines through the darkened varnish. Refinished: $2300-$2500.

Close-up detail of the carved and fluted column of the china closet described above.

Left: Small curio cabinet with a mirrored curio above its center carved door; with bowed glass curio cases. Shown unrestored. $800-$900.

Superb china/curio cabinet with carved crest, arched top, shaped doors, and carved lion heads, which frame the glass-enclosed mirrored curio shelves. The lower portion contains four drawers with carved fronts, flanked by carved lion-head corner posts standing on claw feet. $6000-$7000.

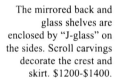

The mirrored back and glass shelves are enclosed by "J-glass" on the sides. Scroll carvings decorate the crest and skirt. $1200-$1400.

Lion head guards the door of the small curio cabinet.

Crystal combination; 70 inches wide by 89 inches tall with three carved crests. Center shaped mirror is divided by a shelf with circular mirrors to each side above glass-enclosed china cabinets. The triple drawers are bowed as is the decorated cabinet below. Solid quartersawn in it's original color and finish. Excellent item. $9500-$10,000.

Above, right: China server curio cabinet with hooded gallery supported by carved griffins. Double china closets with glass shelves and mirrored back are set to each side of a center serving surface with vertical serpentine drawers and bombayed cabinet below. Solid quartersawn and veneer. Shown in unrestored condition. Restored: $7500-$8000.

Detail of china server curio cabinet: hooded gallery supported by griffins.

China closet sideboard with its full width shelf below the carved crest. The bowed glass curio cabinet stands beside the serving area, which is backed by an oval, beveled mirror. The top drawer is cylindrical above the carved cabinet door. A second bowed curio cabinet is provided at the lower left. Solid quartersawn and veneers. $5000-$5500.

Cozy Kitchen

Check the Clock

Advertised as a "Fancy Cabinet Clock," an ornamental clock was often placed on a wall shelf for easy viewing. Eight-day movements struck every hour and half hour, and were adjusted every eight days. This one shows a shapely outline and incised carvings. The pendulum swings behind the reverse-painted glass enclosure. $300-$375.

Hello, Hello...Telephone

A real operator takes your number on this wall telephone, and then she listens. Three rings for Aunt Bertie, down the street. $400-$500.

Spring Cleaning

Bissell's "Grand Rapids Cyco Bearing Carpet Sweeper," advertised in the 1908 Sears Catalog as the best known and most widely sold sweeper in the world. It contains the famous Bissell broom action, anti-raveling collector brush ends, dust-proof axle, tubes, the new improved Bissell's ball socket, and every other desirable feature necessary in the first class sweeper. Made from the best selected cabinet woods in an assortment of attractive finishes. Has improved braid furniture protector encircling the wheels outside case, our everlasting pure bristle brush; both panels open at once by an easy pressure of the finger. Fully guaranteed. Weight, boxed 9.5 pounds. Sears originally priced it at $2.50. This one still works; one in a collection of sweepers. $300 - $325.

Well designed, functional waste can has a wide, open top and slatted sides. The manufacturer's decal remains, but is too faded to read. $150-$200.

The quartersawn umbrella stand currently holds a twisted, glass cane. $200-$250.

Forever Country—Drop-Leaf Style

If Oak Could Talk

A folded letter, handwritten in ink on yellowed paper found in the slides of a similar table reads:

Every time I think of you my heart flops up and down like a churn dasher. Sensations of intelligible joy caper around me like young goat's [sic] on a tin roof and thrill me like Spanish needles pierce a pair of greasy trousers. As a gosling swimming with delight in a mud puddle so I splash in the sea of glory when I think of you.

You stand before me.... I reached out to you like I would to a beautiful blue butterfly making ready to perch on the bean of my greatest grandfather.

When I first beheld your angelic perfection, my brain whirled like a bumblebee under a glass tumbler. My eyes stand open like a cellar door in the country and I left [sic] up my attentions to catch the silvery accents of your voice. I drink of the sweet infection of my love as a thirsty man swalloweth a schooner of beer.

You are fairer than a mud turtle, sweeter than Yankee doughnuts fixed in maple syrup. You are candy-kisses, raisins in a pound cake, all put together. My love for you is stronger than ten year old cheese. I am dying to pour out the living eloquence of my love ... If these remarks enable you to see the inside of my soul and me to win the affection of your incomparable womanhood, I should be as happy as a woodpecker in a cherry tree or a roach in a dirty sink. Yours forever and one day more.

(Unsigned)

How's that for a talking table?

Five turned legs support the top of this drop leaf extension table. Table measures 24 inches by 46 inches closed, but this one is oval when its leaves are pulled up, and can be extended further by three leaves inserted in the center.

Country Armchairs—Rest a While

This bar room armchair has a pressed design around the handgrip, bentwood arms, and solid seat. Spline is inserted in seat for strength to deter splitting. Comfortable. $200-$250.

Bentwood arms and "V" spindles accentuate this armchair. One of a set of ten originating from a Masonic lodge meeting room. Original caned seats have been replaced by leather for better durability. Shown in "as found" condition. Restored, each $300.

Barrel chair with round seat and back. Unusual looking, but not a strong construction.

Four-slat ladderback Queen Anne style armchair. $200-$300.

Cupboards for Country Cooking

Unusual in its size, this hotel model kitchen cupboard offers wonderful storage in its 54-inch width and its large pullout porcelain work surface. $2500-$2800.

Country kitchen combination center kitchen cupboard with its glass enclosed top and pullout porcelain is flanked by its coordinating storage cabinets which stand next to but independently of the center cabinet. Label reads: "High Furniture Company, High Point, North Carolina. Ship to The Friend Furniture. Co., Morgantown, PA." $2200-$2400.

Country noodleboard cupboard with zinc lined dry sink, double door storage compartments, many drawers, pullout cutting board, and pullout bins offers wonderful kitchen usage. $2200-$2500.

Very useful and decorative, this country cupboard shows its original etched glass cupboard doors, pullout cutting board, and many storage areas. $2500-$2800.

Circa 1920 kitchen cupboard with its original label: "J. B. Van Sciver Co., Camden, N.J." $1200-$1500.

Maximum storage and counter space with this 48-inch cabinet. The base cabinet drawer design gives maximum storage. A molding around the top prevents items from falling. Good idea. $1500-$1700.

Very rare in its styling, this Tippee-Canoe cabinet is designed with double, center meeting, horizontal tamboured rolling doors enclosing its cabinets. The base cabinet also is enclosed by a rolling tamboured door. $2200-$2500.

135

From cabinet at left: Original paper inserts remain intact, showing the *Good Housekeeping* seal of approval.

Immaculately preserved kitchen cabinet remains in its darkened varnish, having developed a rich patina. $2300-$2500.

Detail of tiny teapots showing through glass panes, from photo above.

Small scale, 42-inch wide, sideboard designed for a kitchen area. The beveled mirror is shaded, but the crest shines bright with its feathered carvings; shelf supports are scroll carved with claw feet. Stamped in black ink: "From: Dugan & Fry, Allentown, PA." $1400-$1500.

Iceboxes

Opened doors show the insides of the Leonard refrigerator.

This Leonard one-piece porcelain-lined refrigerator made in Grand Rapids, Michigan, by the Grand Rapids Refrigerator Company, is nice, with its porcelain interior and immaculate condition. Patent label reads: "September 20, 1910, through May 24, 1921, Trademark registered." $1500-$1700.

Label from the Leonard refrigerator.

Apartment-sized lift-top icebox, most desirable in decorating smaller spaces. $800-$1000.

Casual Country Stands and Stools

This set of library steps are handy around the house or as a plant stand. $275-$300.

Two straight-grained country-style stands. Left is square everywhere, stamped underneath "Made by W. J. Abele; Nov. 3, 1939." $200-$250. Right has an octagonal top and column on a square base. $175-$200.

Fold-away seating is attached to this telephone table. One lifts the rear of the seat and it folds snugly underneath the table. $350-$375.

Straight slats form the square of this umbrella stand. A metal drip tray is inside. Currently used as a tall fern planter. $150-$175.

Tall stand fits in a corner making a nice curio shelf. Notice the pins down the side that hold the shelves in place, and add interest to the sides. $350-$400.

Early oak kitchen wood box has three compartments with lift-up lids to hold the kindling sizes necessary to start the needed wood-stove fire. Perhaps, it also served as a resting spot for the farmer to recline after lunch. He may have used the raised slanted compartment for a headrest. Not comfortable, but life was not comfortable on the farms at that time. Box is 74 inches long by 17 inches deep and 44 inches tall at the head.$400 - $500.

Fantasy Bedrooms
Matching Bedroom Sets

The bedroom is the most personal of interior spaces to be found in any house. Few bedrooms serve as sitting rooms as they once did, although one cannot say that rooms for sleeping should not also be used for reading, sewing, and other quiet pursuits. One could add pretty single chairs, parlor tables, rockers, etc., to the decor of any bedroom.

Beautiful three-piece bedroom set in quartersawn solid and selected oak veneer. The bombay of the headboard is carried through on the top drawers of the dresser and washstand. The lower portions of each chest are slightly bowed to give a rounded appearance. The carved crest of the bed is duplicated on the dresser mirror frame and on the washstand's cover. Truly a beautiful set. $3500-$4000.

A perfect night stand, this small cabinet holds a pretty lamp and radio, and has a drawer and compartment. Everything in one! $350-$400.

Solid quartersawn, 24 inches round, parlor table with large turned legs and glass ball and talon claw feet glistening in the light. $600-$700.

Below: This bed is part of an elegant three-piece set made by the Burt Brothers furniture manufacturers. Pictured here is a high bed bearing a crescent-shaped carved decoration, duplicated on head and footboard. A carved "shell" decorates the crest. Footboard is rolled, carved, and claw-footed. Label attached to back reads: "From BURT BROS., Philadelphia." (More of the set is shown to the right and on page 142.) Set: $4500-$5000.

Set into a corner, this music cabinet gives drawer and cabinet storage and holds a pretty lamp. $450-$550.

A piece from the Burt set, this solid, quartersawn, shapely dresser mirror matches the design of the carved bed.

141

This washstand chest matches the Burt dresser. The shapely, carved towel bar looks so nice.

The high bed is part of the D. Y. Mowday set. It is decorated with a carved center crest, multi-dimensional panels and moldings and a variety of incised carving. Notice "Z-Z-Z-Z-Z's" across the top, as if to signify "sleep." Beautiful rails extend the bed.

FROM
BURT BROS.,
FURNITURE MANUFACTURERS
2000 to 2014 SOUTH NINTH STREET,
PHILADELPHIA, PA.

Detail of label found on the Burt bedroom set described previously.

The dresser matches the bed exactly and stands tall with its beveled mirror. Every drawer is stamped by the maker: "D. Y. Mowday, Cabinetmaker, Norristown, PA".

The upholstered backrest of this pretty settee is surrounded by carved quartersawn oak panels. The flowing arms are decorated by stick 'n' ball spindles. A nice bedroom addition. The beautiful Mowday bedroom set is an Eastlake-style of exceptional quality in tightly grained quartersawn oak. Set: $5000-$5500.

142

The washstand stands tall with the other Mowday pieces.

"Bumblebee" hardware on the raised panel drawer fronts.

The D. Y. Mowday maker's stamp is in every drawer.

This dresser shows a serpentined front with paneled side. The carved mirror frame matches the crest of the bed to the left.

Absolutely stunning with rolled, heavily scroll-carved head and footboards; wild open-grain patterns. This bed is part of the same set as the dresser on the right.

Stunning princess dresser with serpentined front. Tall beveled mirror with rolled and scrolled frame to match the set. This goes with the bed and washstand at the bottom, left and right.

Another super piece, this washstand goes with the dresser on page 143, bottom right. The top drawer is serpentined to match the dresser. The carved mirror frame duplicates the crest of the set. Placement on each side of the bed in this lovely set, the pair provide night stands and visually frame the bed headboard with their mirrors. Set: $6000-$7000.

Mirrored washstand matches the set. The mirror harp carries the rolls and scroll of the other pieces. Set: $7000-$8000.

Wild quartersawn grain patterns swirl on the rolls and scrolls of this tall bed.

Eight foot tall quartersawn bed with molded top and deeply carved floral crest with arched inset. Excellent quality.

The headboard is elaborately carved with winged griffins guarding the crest over two angels sheltering a lady. Two more griffins sit below the large finials to each side. The significance of this specific design is not known. The bed is 65 inches wide, the headboard is 77 inches tall, and the footboard is 42 inches tall.

Detail of crest of eight foot tall bed.

Dresser follows the same lines as the bed. The tall mirror frame duplicates the carved headboard. Both dresser and washstand have brown marble tops. Set $15,000-$18,000.

Detail of top right carved headboard.

Gigantic in its stature, quartersawn panels are filled to capacity with beautiful scroll patterns. Huge double doors close to the center post with carved griffins guarding. Three huge claw feet support this armoire as it reaches high to the ceiling. It is a sight to behold! The armoire is 95 inches tall by 78 inches wide by 21.5 inches deep. Set: Value is currently undetermined.

Incredible quartersawn, six drawer high chest with its molded top, lion head columns and carved drawer fronts with carved lion head drawer pulls. Heavy recessed paneled sides are carved to match armoire. 70 inches tall by 47 inches wide by 23 inches deep.

Base of armoire showing carved drawer pulls, with incised carved molded base set upon big claw feet. Same carvings on high chest.

Side view of armoire with its heavy molded top, carved panels and griffin side posts. These carvings are duplicated on the sides of the high chest.

Bedroom Pairs

Two piece matching set includes dresser and high chest; a desirable combination. Straight grained solid oak with bowed top drawers, carved mirror frames with rolls supported by turned posts. Set: $2200-$2500.

Pretty two-piece Eastlake style set, including high bed and matching dresser bearing the same carved crest. Dresser has incised flowing leaf carvings on each drawer face. Set $2200 -$2400.

Pretty two piece set with dresser and matching washstand. Incised "flowing leaf" patterns decorate all the drawers. Pair: $1400-$1600.

Similar in design, these two pieces are solid with straight fronts, slightly bowed top drawers, shaped mirror and harp with a carved crest. Pair: $1500.

Victorian-style, white marble-topped dresser with glove boxes and its matching washstand in close-grained oak; made to resemble this style in walnut. It was offered as a budget, look-alike, substitute. Many, who had seen this set, remember it as they let it slip away to another. Set: $2000-$2200.

This washstand goes with the Victorian-style dresser.

Beds of Sweet Dreams

Full size, quartersawn, short oak bed with center carved crest and rolled headboard. $800-$900.

Outstanding Eastlake-style tall bed with its carved crest and butterprint carved panels. $2500-$2700.

Incredible, quartersawn, eight-foot-tall bed extensively carved in asymmetrical patterns across the head and footboards. $5000-$5500.

Tall, straight grained oak bed with heavy scrolled center crest flowing to the side posts with its decorated rolled footboard. $1400-$1500.

Beautifully decorated, this rolled and scroll carved bed has rolls at the side posts too, making it very graceful. Its shortened height has not hurt the beauty a bit. $1200-$1400.

Charming and modestly decorated with incised carvings of Eastlake style. The crest resembles a sunburst with radiating rays. $700-$900.

Awaiting refinishing, this tall bed shows a wide carved, decorated crest. As shown: $600-$700.

Short, carved headboard with raised panel and dimensional Eastlake style carvings. $700-$800.

Tall oak bed with beautifully carved crest and flowing lines. Matching dresser and washstand not shown. Set: $2500-$2700.

Heavy, solid quartersawn tall bed with carved raised panel decorations. $1800-$2000.

Tall, straight grained, oak bed with raised panel headboard and footboard. A high carved crest crowns the headboard. $1600. Left: Set of four very basic T-back solid seated dining chairs. Set of four: $600-$700. Right: Exceptional rocking chair with extra tall back, turned rabbit ears, spindles, quadruple pressings including skirt, bentwood arms, and caned seat. $500-$600.

High Chests with Tall Character

Giant, solid quartersawn, "lock-side" high chest with graduated drawer sizes. The fancy board with its incised leaf carvings stands across the top. A vertical hinged flap, when engaged, overlaps the drawer edges and all are locked at once. Quality shows in the paneled sides and large drawers that glide like butter. $1400-$1600.

Tall with its shaped beveled mirror, the top two drawers bow forward above the lower three accented by rope twists. Nice style with paneled sides in straight grained oak. $1200 - $1500.

Stunning, quartersawn, bow front, high chest with thick, raised-panel sides. Leaf carvings cover the 1.5-inch thick drawer faces. The mirror harp bears acanthus carvings supported by fluted columns with brass, flame finials. The chest top edge is gadrooned for added eloquence. Corner posts are carved with leaves and scrolls. Extremely heavy of quality, high-grade lumber. $3500-$3700.

Outstanding Empire-style chifferobe of solid quartersawn and grain matched oak veneers. The windowpane closet door radiates its vivid patterns. The picture framed beveled mirror stands above its petite chest of drawers to the right. A full width drawer is provided across the bottom. Wonderful quality and character. $1200-$1400.

Huge, 50 inches wide by 50 inches high by 25.5 inches deep, quartersawn high chest with beautiful grain patterns traveling across the face of the six large drawers. $1500-$1700.

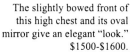

The slightly bowed front of this high chest and its oval mirror give an elegant "look." $1500-$1600.

Six drawers appear to be twelve on this Eastlake-style chest with double applied panels on each drawer. A tall fancy board stands across the top. Paneled side give strength. $1800-$2000.

Six graduated drawers are decorated with "Eastlake Butterprint" carving as is the fancy board at the top: 35 inches wide by 21 inches deep by 54 inches tall plus an 8-inch splashboard. $1800-$2000.

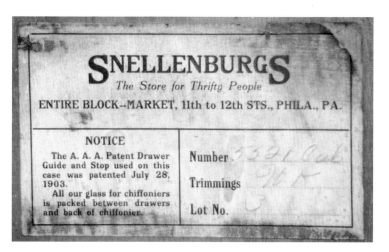

Immaculate darkened
varnish, this
serpentined two over
four drawer high chest
with its oval mirror is
quite elegant. Original
label reads:
"Snellenburgs,"
Philadelphia, PA., with
a patented drawer guide
of 1903. As shown:
$800-$1000.

Stunning Eastlake-style six drawer high chest with
incised carved drawers and fancy board at top; paneled
sides. $1800-$2000.

Solid, straight grained, petite high chest originally
purchased in 1929 with a matching vanity. $500-$600.

Outstanding six drawer Eastlake high chest with carved drawer faces and intricate openwork gallery. Original label reads: "Michelsen & Hoppe, Manufacturers of Furniture, N. Water St. Rochester, N.Y." $2000-$2200.

Double offset bonnet boxes highlight this handsome mirrored high chest of solid quartersawn oak. $1600-$1800.

Left: Double hat boxes with their carved doors take your eye up to the horizontal oval mirror standing above this high chest. $1600-$1800.

Right: Serpentined bonnet chest with its quartersawn grain and shaped beveled mirror is quite elegant. $1200-$1500.

Scrolled carvings decorate the drawer faces of this tall, mirrored high chest. Shown dusty and unrefinished. $1000-$1200.

Around the corner is a sitting room with oval coffee table and a fancy parlor table.

Heavily painted in this photograph, this serpentined, drop top high chest style is of great popularity. Extensive work is needed before the beauty will show. When refinished: $2200-$2400.

Swell front high chest with center carved bonnet box and four small glove drawers. The shapely mirror and its carved frame stand tall above the interesting chest. Shown dusty and unrefinished. $1200-$1300.

Solid quartersawn Empire-style high chest with six drawer levels plus a double bonnet box. The waved sides frame the tall chest nicely. $1800-$2000.

Delightful Dressers

Pleasant to look at, but not exactly what you see. The dresser is a convertible! The serpentined drawer unit pivots 180 degrees to expose a liquor cabinet hideaway. Directions say: "Dresser must rest equally on all four legs." Patent was applied for and pending by the Hartley Manufacturing Company, Chicago. $1600-$1700.

Here we see the dresser with its liquor cabinet swinging out and fully exposed.

Pretty serpentined dresser with its tall shaped mirror and carved harp. $800-$900.

Exceptionally wide, the three top drawers are cylindrical over two serpentined drawers. The large mirror frame shows a roll with carving. Solid quartersawn and veneer. $1400-$1500.

Bureau-Top Mirrors

The oval mirror over the swelled front of this dresser gives it elegance. $1400-$1500.

The 21-inch by 14-inch oval frame of this 30-inch tall, bureau-top mirror swings in its bowfront stand; 18 inches wide by 6.5 inches at the corners with two small drawers and tiny feet. Mint original condition. $1500-$1800.

Dressers for Your Princess

Fabulous triple mirrored princess dresser. The carved crest crowns the mirror frame of the center beveled mirror. Two vertical elongated oval mirrors are hinged to each side to adjust the viewing. The mirror harp is tastefully decorated with carved lilies at the top and claw feet at the bottom where it meets the dresser. Quartersawn oak grain radiates beneath each mirror. The chest indents at center, housing a carved hidden drawer. The full width drawers beneath follow the same contours. The corners are columns standing on carved claw feet. Solid quartersawn oak and oak veneers. Stunning! $3000-$3500.

Open, ribbon carving decorates the crest of this outstanding mirror. Carved, winged ladies balance torch-like, turned, fluted columns with flame finials upon their heads, providing the support for the mirror screws. 36 inches tall by 26 inches wide in original varnish. $2900-$3000.

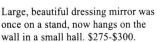

Unusual, quartersawn princess-vanity with its tall, oval mirror above the concave serpentine of the two-drawer chest. A shell carved fan provides the transition between drawers allowing space for the knees while sitting. Shown in clean, original, but lackluster finish. $1500-$1600.

Large, beautiful dressing mirror was once on a stand, now hangs on the wall in a small hall. $275-$300.

Tall, oval-mirrored princess dresser with crested mirror frame and carved harp over serpentined drawers. $900-$1000.

Bow-front, princess dresser with its tall oval mirror and "S"-curled harp sits around the corner from coordinating high chest. $1100-$1200.

Volusion vanity with its tall center mirror flanked to each side by elevated glove drawers and hatbox over a low chest of drawers $1600 -$1800.

Pretty princess dresser with serpentined top drawers and tall, shaped mirror. $800-$900.

Exceptionally wide princess dresser with its large, crested beveled mirror over a serpentined chest standing on claw feet. $1200-$1400.

Cheval Dressers

Beautiful cheval-dresser with its oval mirror and ribbon-carved frame above the low chest of drawers. A bonnet box and glove drawers are provided to the right. $1600-$1800.

Tall, mirrored cheval dresser with carved mirror frame and decorated bonnet box to right. $1600-$1800.

The carved crest crowns the tall mirror of this cheval dresser overlooking its low chest. $1400-$1500.

Romantic Armoires

This armoire is magnificent with its tall, wide, carved crest above the double mirrored doors. Reeded columns stand to each side. The base is serpentined containing two drawers. $3500-$4000.

Left: A quartersawn beauty with its carved, shaped, beveled mirrored doors enclosing the closet, set upon a double-draw base. $3000-$3500.

Right: In excess of 8 feet tall with its crest, this elaborate, mirrored armoire shows rolls, scrolls, and feathered carvings. The drawer base has two barrel drawers and a full width serpentined drawer. $3800-$4000.

Washstands

Left: Tall and gorgeous, this mirrored with its rolled and scrolled mirror makes a beautiful accent anywhere. $1500-$1700.
Below: Soft curves follow the front and sides of this wide, graceful washstand. $700-$800.

Bold in appearance; solid quartersawn washstand with its towel bar. $750-$850.

Pretty, Eastlake-style washstand decorated with incised leaf carvings. $600 - $700.

A washstand without its towel bar makes a great night stand. $400 - $500.

Basic model washstand in its classic style. $400-$500.

Small Chests

Quartersawn blanket chest, 37 inches long by 19 inches deep by 21 inches high, with incised carved end panels and long tongued griffin; a floral motif decorates the side panels. The top is carved with an incised sunburst. $1500-$1700.

Serpentine three drawer princess chest; quartersawn veneer with shapely legs. $400-$450.

Country chestnut blanket chest gives great storage. $500-$600.

Bow-front two drawer princess chest with claw feet; quartersawn veneer. $400-$450.

Two drawer, solid straight grained bachelor's chest decorated by a tiny pressed pattern and a small carving. Once was part of a cheval dresser, it has become a conveniently low storage chest. $400-$500.

This three drawer chest is undecorated except for its grain patterns and grooved drawers. Nice plain lines. $400-$450.

Solid straight grained three drawer lowboy chest with incised Eastlake decoration. Very popular size and style with many useful purposes as well as being decorative. $450-$550.

Solid quartersawn two-over-two chest of drawers with fancy drawer pulls. Once it had a mirror, but now serves as a storage chest. $600 -$700.

Solid quartersawn, slightly bowed, two-over-two chest of drawers. $600-$700.

Vanity Dressers for Her

Incredible vanity and matching chair. The oval mirrors on both items are adjustable four ways for excellent viewing. Two thin chests of small drawers with a cabinet on the right support the drop-well vanity top. A small knob above the center drawer pulls a jewelry tray forward for ease of selection. The pedestal swivel chair has an open carved back. It stands on a platform base with claw feet. Set: $4500-$5000.

Beautiful vanity with shapely beveled mirror, carved detailing and fine delicate legs. $900-$1000.

1929 vanity model with tri-fold mirrors, drop center, two drawers, and straight legs with brass cuffs. Its matching high chest went to another home. $600-$700.

Elegant oval mirrored vanity dresser with finely-shaped legs and soft flowing lines. $900-$1000.

Stunning vanity with its thin necked oval mirror frame and mirror. $1000-$1100.

Undecorated, except for graining, the curvature of the triple mirror is its beauty. Label reads: "Atlas Furniture Company, Made in Jamestown, New York." $800-$900.

Empire style, triple mirrored vanity in quartersawn veneer. $700-$800.

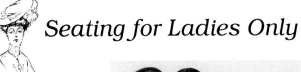
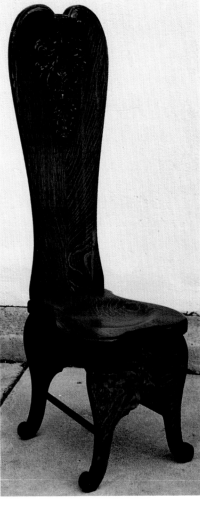

Absolutely stunning tall chair with its carved back and shaped contoured seat and unique design; this is a focal point anywhere. $850-$900.

Single drawer vanity with two drawers below, large mirror, carved crest, fine legs. $1200-$1400.

Outstanding with its large, shaped mirror, its fine French lines, and its jewelry boxes. $1600-$1800.

167

168

Variety of ladies chairs used for vanities, desks, and bedroom chairs. $95-$250.

Specialties for Him

For His Vanity, Shaving Stands

For His Jewelry

A sweet lion, he is, as he lays on the lid of this 17 inch long by 11 inch deep jewelry box. This lion lays 8 inches off the table with his head at 14 inches. No small lion here. Original finish is well preserved, as is the interior. Mint condition: $2500-$2700.

Left: A fully rotating, round, beveled mirror stands above its round, 6-inch high quartersawn veneer cabinet supported by a round, tapered column with curled feet. $900-$1000.

Right: The unusual triangular-shaped beveled mirror is duplicated in the shape of its shallow cabinet supported by a pedestal balanced by flared legs. $1400-$1500.

The tray on the inside lifts out with a 1 inch space below to hide items. Rosewood and satinwood inlaid lids with ivory knobs secure several jewelry compartments.

Velvet lined areas receive rings, wrist watches, and cuff links. Center compartment is inlaid with a monogrammed wreath. A tiny tray pulls out to receive your current day's jewelry selections. Mint condition.

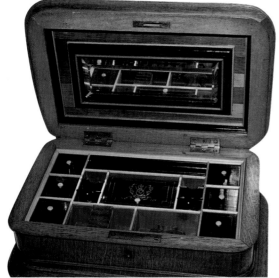

Right: The round, rotating, beveled mirror stands above the bowed drawer cabinet of this shaving stand. Tall, straight legs with a tiny shelf support the cabinet. $850-$900.

Far right: Standing 62 inches tall, a pierced panel at the back and long, tapered, fluted legs, at front, support the small shelf and cabinet of the oval mirrored shaving stand. $1400-$1500.

Library

Shed a Little Light

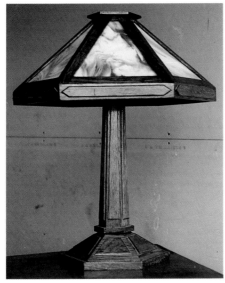

Arts and crafts lamp in its beautiful patina; 26.5 inches tall with six panels. The 12- inch base supports the 21-inch wide oak shade. No signature. $7700-$900.

Definitely masculine, this lamp is supported by a quartersawn raised-panel 15-inch square base with 5-inch extensions at each corner to accommodate a set of four full-bodied, carved, male lions. $1200-$1500.

The reverse-painted glass shade hangs suspended in its oak rope-twisted frame; 26 inches tall and 15.5 inches at the widest; 11.25 at the top. An open-carved crest stands between the finials. Signed: "Paine Furniture, Boston, Mass." $900-$1100.

Bookcases

Absolutely incredible matched pair of giant sectional bookcases with drawers in bases. Standing 75.5 inches tall, each is 40 inches wide and 17 inches deep. Vibrant, quartersawn grain radiates across the drawer faces; raised panels decorate the end of each unit. Pair: $5000-$6000.

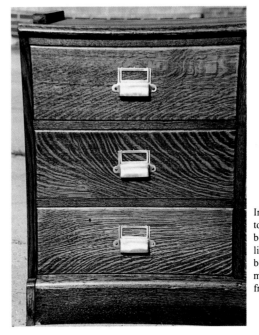

In this picture, the top part of one bookcase has been lifted off, and the bottom drawers may be seen in frontal view.

Small scale revolving bookcase is perfect for small books, cassettes, videos, and compact discs. $800-$900.

Globe-Wernieke "Art-Mission" sectional bookcase with outstanding style. Four cases tall, each one is of a graduated height. Original labels are all perfectly intact. $1500-$1600.

Detail showing original label of the Globe-Wernieke Company's Art-Mission bookcase.

Beautiful three-high sectional bookcase, signed Maceys; 34 inches wide, 14 inches tall by 12.5 inches deep, for big books. $1500-$1600.

An exceptional pair of three-high Globe-Wernieke sectional bookcases, identical except for one which has a drawer base. Pair: $2000-$2200.

Three-high sectional bookcase with sculptured top and drawer made by the Gunn Bookcase Company. $1100-$1200.

Cutest two high, sectional, claw-footed bookcase, labeled R. A. Macey and Company. $500-$600.

Most unusual, this tall document chest is enclosed by its full length tamboured, rolled front door. Eleven drawers are revealed with the roll partially lifted. It sits beside a five-high Globe-Wernieke sectional bookcase. File:$1200-$1400. Bookcase: $1200-$1400.

Most desirable two-high sectional bookcase with sculptured top and base. Original label reads:"Humphrey, Sectional Bookcase." Wild grain quartersawn oak. $500-$600.

This double glass-door bookcase has great character. It is guarded a each corner by open mouthed carved lions. $1800-$2200.

Simplistic in style, this bookcase with its large glass paneled doors is most desirable for display of books or treasures. $1500-$1700.

Detail of one carved lion that decorates the double glass-door bookcase.

Stately in character, this
stepback bookcase offers
great display and drawer
storage.$1800-$1900.

Solid quartersawn
Empire-style double
glass-door bookcase.
$1500-$1600.

Detail of sculptured corner and column.

Quartersawn sectional desk/bookcase combination
in original darkened varnish. Signed: Macey's.
Three drawers are provided; two below the desk
top and one under the bookcase. $1200 -$1300.

Library Desks and Tables

Top left: Beautiful, elegant, quartersawn desk with wonderful curves and shaped legs that stand on claw feet. $2500-$2600.

Top right: "S"-curled legs gracefully support the top of this Empire-style library desk. $700-$800.

Forty-eight inches square in size, this massive library desk is decorated with fine scrolled carving on all sides of its apron. Huge claw feet support the table. $1200-$1400.

Most substantial, this 42 inches wide by 96 inches long library table houses three large drawers with carved pulls; it has a straight grained top. Five large, turned, tapered legs support this work space—so useful for many things. $2200-$2500.

This oval empire style library desk has unusual design with platform base and claw feet. $1200-$1400.

Soft curves and quartersawn grain patterns show on the contoured top of this library desk with its shapely legs and shelf. $800-$900.

Talon claw and ball feet add interest to the clean lines of this quartersawn library desk. Otherwise plain but of good quality. $700-$800.

This large, quartersawn, 60-inch oval library table shows a leaf and scroll carved skirt below the gadrooned edge of the table top. Four large, fluted column legs with capitals support the table connected by the shaped stretcher shelf. Huge claw feet support the columns. $5500-$5800.

Small scale in design, this library desk is most useful. $500-$600.

The oval top of this library desk is supported by its "S"-curled legs. $900-$1000.

A shaped, heavily carved apron decorates this library desk, which has shapely legs with carved talon claw and ball feet. $1500-$1600.

Incredible twisted legs and stretchers decorate this library desk with its large glass ball and talon claw feet. $1500-$1600.

Each end of this large library table is completely covered with leaf and scroll carvings. $1800-$2000.

Quartersawn library desk with its leather top, supported by turned legs. The shelf below wears a carved floral decoration. $1200-$1300.

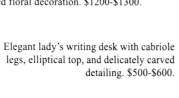

Elegant lady's writing desk with cabriole legs, elliptical top, and delicately carved detailing. $500-$600.

Office Efficiency

Outstanding Rolltop Desks

Top left: Beautiful cabinetry is exhibited in this 66-inch wide, 52-inch tall, "S"-rolltop with its quartersawn raised-panel construction, carved drawer pulls, and rope-twisted rolltop handles. Maker: Midland Manufacturing Co., Chicago, Illinois. $11,000 - $12,000.
Bottom left: Under the rolltop, a fabulous interior offers numerous drawers and "cubbies." Below, double doors pivot open to reveal a hidden storage area.
Top right: The tamboured rolltop rolls forward, curling to reach 42 inches deep.
Bottom right: Beautiful graining radiates "quality."

"Perpetual calendar" desk set including a double inkwell stand with bottles having oak lids, a blotter, a letter opener, and an oak clip to keep items tidy. $300-$400.

Massive, with its high upholstered headrest, and 3-inch side posts, this leather-covered swivel desk chair complements the rolltop on the previous page, with matching carvings. Maker: Chicago Chair Co., Chicago, Illinois. $3500-$3700.

This exceptional lady's quartersawn desk is 35 inches wide, 49 inches high, and 30 inches deep. It has an "S"-rolltop, raised panels, an unusually contoured desk enclosure, shaped drawers, gallery top, and graceful lines. Immaculate original condition including locks and keys. Maker: Shelbyville Desk Co., Shelbyville, Indiana. $3800-$4200.

Decorative and useful, this fancy, round, quartersawn waste basket has caned sides and rope-twisted trimmings in its immaculate original finish including original caning. $650 - $750.

The interior features are a good indication of the quality of any desk. Most important when evaluating a rolltop desk. The more detailed, the better the desk.

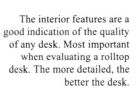

Very basic model, 48-inch wide, rolltop desk shows a low slope to the roll, straight grained recessed panels with drawer and cabinet storage. Interior is minimal with cubbies. $1100 - $1200.

Quartersawn, raised panel 42-inch wide rolltop desk with carved drawer pulls and a quantity of cubbies and drawers. $2700-$3000.

Incredible, quartersawn, raised panel "partners' desk." At 60 inches by 72 inches, this desk gives ample workspace for two individuals simultaneously. $3500-$3800.

Purposely patterned, the quartersawn veneered top is herringbone. Wonderful!

Classic, quartersawn 48-inch, raised panel, flat top office desk. Nice quality. $1400-$1500.

Of unique design, this heavy duty mission-style desk offers a pullout writing surface with storage and shelf. A perfect computer station? $600-$700.

Office Chairs

Standing tall, this technical easel, known as "tricky easel" has many adjustable positions. Notice the notched brackets at top and bottom. For making the adjustments. Signed: "Technical Supply Co.; Sole Manufacturers, Scranton, PA." Patented June 25, l901. $200-$250.

One of a set of four heavy duty, comfortable office armchairs. Manufactured by Hale & Kilburn Manufacturing Company, Philadelphia, Pa. The set: $1000.

Matching swivel desk chair. $450-$500.

Quartersawn armchair with its smooth rounded back and sculptured solid seat. $300-350.

Quartersawn armchair: headrest is supported by six arrowback slats. The arms graceful slope supported by large turned spindles. Turned rungs and flared legs. $375-$425.

Plain, but stylish and comfortable, this pair of armchairs have solid, sculptured seats for comfort. Pair: $500.

Basic model school teacher's chair. $125-$150.

Scriber's swivel desk chair offers height and a comfortable foot rest ring. $300-$400.

High-back, upholstered swivel desk chair, manufactured by The Sikes Company, Philadelphia, Pa. $900-$1000.

Tall, arrowback, pressed-back solid seated desk chair with its heart shaped pressing. $600-$700.

This is a detail of the tall, arrowback desk chair.

Low back, solid-seated swivel desk chair is most comfortable. $500- $600.

Tall rabbit ears frame the pressed decoration of this cane-seated swivel desk chair. $500-$600.

Pressed-back, spindled, cane seated swivel desk chair with bentwood arms. $500-$600.

Detail of arrowback "Tree of Life swivel desk chair.

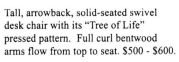

Tall, arrowback, solid-seated swivel desk chair with its "Tree of Life" pressed pattern. Full curl bentwood arms flow from top to seat. $500 - $600.

Basic model, solid, straight-cut oak, swivel desk chair. $300-$350.

Filing Cabinets

Quartersawn, armless, secretary's swivel desk chair. $300-$350.

Incredible engineering blueprint flat-filing case. Ten drawers housed in two units are each 64 inches wide by 36.5 inches front to back and 3 inches deep on the inside. The cabinet is free standing with recessed panels on three sides measuring 68 inches wide by 39 inches deep by 52 inches tall. After many years in storage with no place to go, it was refinished and has found its home with elated engineers in Toledo, Ohio. Hooray! $3500-$3800.

Office companion cabinet with pull out writing surface, two document drawers, and filing compartments behind double doors, raised panel cabinet. $900-$1000.

Wonderful, stackable office filing unit with storage, double file drawers, eighteen card-file drawers, and an open bookcase. Manufactured by The Yawman and Erbe Manufacturing Company, Rochester, New York. $2000-$2200. (see label at top right)

Quartersawn, combination office filing unit containing a variety of filing drawers, including standard, legal, and flat file sizes. $1500-$1600.

Quartersawn, double filing cabinet with bookcase top, recessed paneled sides and back; 33 inches wide by 25 inches deep by 52 inches tall at setback, and 68 inches overall height. Five sectional units are included. Maker: Yawman & Erbe Manufacturing Company, Rochester, New York. $3000-$3500.

Small Files

Three-drawer, raised-panel document chest with its decorative fittings. $500-$600.

Most useful, this office cabinet provides great storage. Manufactured by Yawman and Erbe Manufacturing Company, Rochester, New York, as noted on metal nameplate. $1500-$1600.

Two-drawer card file, made by Pixley Safe Company, is ideal for today's video cassettes. $200-$250.

Slight "S"-rolltop desk with spindled straight chair. Set: $400-$500.

This six-drawer document chest serves as a great night stand. $450-$500.

This is one of three pint-size styles of office desk and chair sets: "C"-roll desk with T-back swivel desk chair. Signed by The Paris Manufacturing Company. Set: $400-$500.

Flat-top desk with spindled-back swivel desk chair. Set: $300-$400 .

Before You Go

Let me show you my fabulous desk.

Extraordinarily carved drop-front desk, New York; hand made sometime during the last half of the nineteenth century. This beauty stands on four capital carved legs with molded feet. Wonderful craftsmanship is exhibited in the paneled and carved sides. The drop front is elegantly carved and decorated with dentil molding. The masterful crest has two sitting cupids on each side; one plays the lyre and the other reads a book. Two, carved, winged cupids rest on either side of the open acanthus, carved cabochon crest. In untouched original finish, this desk is a rare work of art. A masterpiece, unsigned. $8000-$9000.

The interior is complete, original, and simply elegant with cubbies and drawers.

Watch your step, the parquet floor was recently waxed.

This view shows intricate designs in the oak parlor floor of "Oakbourne," a lovely Victorian home built in 1892 in the Queen Anne revival style. Eastlake decorations prevail, as seen in the newel post. The area of this floor is surrounded by quartersawn raised panel walls, doors, and moldings with stained-glass windows.

GLOSSARY

Acanthus leaf. Adapted from the more-or-less ragged leaf of the acanthus plant. The leaf is the distinguishing mark of the Corinthian capital.

Applied carving/decoration. Ornamentation crafted separately, then attached to achieve decoration, as applied scroll carving.

Apron. A narrow strip of decorated or plain wood adjoining the base of cabinet bodies, chair seats, table tops, etc., extending between the tops of leg or feet brackets. Often used to conceal underframing.

Armchair. Compared with the ordinary chair, the arm chair is larger and more conducive to repose.

Arm support. The vertical or curved upright supporting the front end of chair arms.

Armoire. Synonymous with "wardrobe" as a large cupboard originally used for storing clothing.

Arrowback. Flattened spindles, often bent for comfort, having arrow-pointed end shapes, spaced to form chair backs.

Atlas. A supporting pillar designed in the shape of a man.

Beading. Carving resembling beads in a line as decoration.

Bed. An article of furniture upon which one rests or sleeps.

Bedroom suite. The basic set consists of a high-back bed, dresser, and washstand. Available in a wide range of styles, qualities, and overall ornateness or lack thereof.

Belter, John Henry. New York City cabinetmaker (1804-1863), considered to have created superb Victorian Rococo pieces.

Bench. An elongated seat, usually intended for several persons, furnished with a back and arms.

Bentwood. A method developed in 1836 by German cabinetmaker Michael Thonet, when he perfected the method of soaking stacks of thin veneer in hot glue to render the wood pliable enough to be molded into bent forms.

Beveled. An edge cut to an angle other than 90 degrees; the inclination that one surface makes with another when not at right angles.

Bombe. An outward swelling, curving, or bulging.

Boxed seat. A form of chair construction showing an apron-like structure beneath the seat that connects the legs, thus "boxing the seat" and strengthening the chair. Often combined with H-rungs set lower on the legs.

Braces. "Hiphuggers." Short bentwood supports attached to the back leg and seat where they meet to provide strength. Found often on pressed-back chairs with single post back legs.

Buffet. A small cupboard or counter for refreshments. Smaller in size than a sideboard with or without a short back.

Bulbous. Having the shape of a bulb. Often used to describe a large, bulging table leg.

Bun feet. A flattened ball or bun shape with slender ankle above.

Cabochon. A plain round or oval surface, convex or concave, enclosed with an ornamentation.

Cabriole. A term applied to legs that swell outward at the upper part or knee and inward at the lower part or ankle. There are many variations with different feet.

Cane. Long, narrow strips of rattan used for the weaving of chair seats and backs.

Caned chair. Where the seat alone or in conjunction with the back is of woven or pressed cane.

Cantilever mirrors. Triple mirrors mounted in such a way that the two outside mirrors are attached by hinges on one side only to allow adjustment toward the center.

Capital. The top of a column.

Cased. Any cabinet-type item of furniture.

Castors. Small wheels set into the feet or base of furniture to allow easier movement. Wood, metal or glass can be used.

Chifferobe. A piece of furniture designed with a closet on one side and a chest of drawers on the other.

China cabinet. A glass enclosed article of furniture designed to house and display glass and dinnerware.

Claw and ball feet. The foot of a leg shaped as a three-toed talon as it envelopes a ball. Seen as metal claws over a crystal ball or as carved claw and ball completely of wood.

Claw foot. The foot of a leg carved in the shape of a lion's paw or sometimes a bear claw. Can be found on all furniture items standing on legs.

Concave. Curving inwardly; opposite of convex.

Concave seat. Where the middle and front of which are lower than the sides to better fit body contours.

Convex. Curving outwardly; opposite of concave.

Cornice. The horizontal molding found at the top on furniture.

Cornice. The top-most decorative ornament on a piece of furniture.

Cross-rail. A horizontal bar in a chair back.

C-scroll. A carving which resembles a "C."

Cupboard. An item of furniture having an enclosed storage area. Often the top has glass doors; the base cabinet has solid doors.

Curio cabinet. A small scale, glass-enclosed article of furniture to house and display a prized collection. Often constructed with a mirrored back and crystal-glass shelves.

Dolphin. A marine animal whose head and body, or head alone, is often used for decorative purposes.

Drop front. As found on a desk being a hinged lid dropping forward to form a writing surface on the underside.

Eastlake-style. In the style of Charles Eastlake.

Eastlake, Charles Locke (1836-1906). An English architect introduced furniture designs possessing simplicity in rectangular shapes. His designs were to be clean, practical, and functional, with old gothic ornamentation and burled walnut trim added to some.

Elements of decoration. These are geometrical lines, ornament, natural foliage, artificial objects, animal and the human figures.

Embellish. To enhance beauty with additional decoration.

Escutcheon. A shaped plate or brass fitting for a keyhole.

Fancy board. A decorative finishing board used on a furniture item that does not have a mirror, such as a buffet or high chest. Similar to a splashboard on a washstand.

Flint, George. New York City cabinetmaker.

Gadroon. A carved molding used mainly on table tops and chair edges.

Gallery. A decorative railing around the tops of furniture.

Gargoyle. A grotesquely carved creature used as an ornament.

Griffin. A chimerical beast having the union of a lion's body with the head and wings of an eagle. The fore extremities may belong to either the lion or the eagle.

Grotesque. Fantastic, often incredibly ugly, monsters produced by the combination of human, animal, and plant organisms.

H-rungs. A design of strengthening rungs attaching the front legs to the back, with a center rung that attaches these to each other across the middle, forming an "H."

Hardware. Metal used on a piece of furniture; drawer pulls, knobs, etc.

Harp. The structure supporting a mirror on a dresser or high chest.

Headpiece. Top-most rail of a chair, plain or fancy.

Horner Bros. New York cabinetmaker.

Hunzinger, George. (1835-1898) One of nineteenth-century America's most innovative and idiosyncratic furniture maker.

Knee. The uppermost part of a cabriole leg.

Ladderback. A chair-back in which a series of horizontal cross rails are used instead of a splat, giving the effect of a ladder.

Laminating. The process involving the steam heating under pressure of 4 to 16 layers of wood to produce greater strength.

Lyre. A decorative motif, selected from the musical instrument of the same name.

Masque. The French word combining "masks" and "caricatures" to describe countenances. The former being the delineation of beautiful faces and the latter being faces grinning, deformed or distorted. Masks and caricatures pass into each other, as clearly expressed by this one word.

Mission-style. The generic term used to describe all the solid, plain, straight-lined oak furniture of strong construction that was manufactured during the early years of the twentieth century.

Molding. A frame or border constructed by shaped lengths of wood.

Morris, William. (1834-1896) An English reformer, poet and interior designer is best known for his invention of the "Morris Armchair".

Morris chair. Reclining armchair invented about 1860 by William Morris.

Motif. The dominant feature manifested in a work.

Music cabinet. An enclosed item of furniture designed for storage of musical supplies; sheet music, etc.

Northwind. A masque depicting a face with cheeks full as if blowing.

Ornamentation. Details added to heighten attractiveness.

Pier mirror. A tall, narrow mirror originally used in a foyer or between two windows.

Pierced. To have cutout areas incorporated in the design as a pierced splat-back on a chair. Also, carved backs with opening within the carved design.

Pilaster. A flat column attached to the face of a plain surface mainly as an ornamental support for an arch, cornice, or other superstructure.

Pressed-back. A decorative design embossed most often on the backs of chairs.

Quartersawn. Lumber taken from the log by first cutting it into four pie-shaped wedges. Each wedge is sliced radially to expose the pith rays running from the center outward, creating a two-tone pattern with curved grain. Furniture of the best quality is quartersawn, which preserves strength and minimizes warping.

Rabbit ears. Name often used in reference to the finials on a pressed-back chair.

Raised panel. The result of a chamfer.
Reeding. Semicircular, straight cuttings resembling reeds. The reverse of fluting.
Recessed panel. The result when cross-members are set into the stiles of a cased furniture item.
Ribbon carved. Carving resembling a ribbon; as a ribbon crest.
Rolltop. Narrow, parallel slats in various shapes, mounted on a flexible backing.
Rolltop desk. A desk having a rolltop, self-storing flexible hood.
Roman chair. An armchair design freely adapted from a style of sixteenth century Italian Renaissance folding X-form.
Rung. A crosspiece connecting cabinet, chair, or table legs, providing structural strength. Sometimes called "stretchers."
Saddle seat. A solid seat shaped to fit the contours of the body.
Scalloped. A series of curves, providing an ornamental edge.
Sculptured seat. Similar to saddle seat.
Serpentine. A front shaped with a waving curve or curves.
Settee. A small scale elongated seat with a back.
Shaving stand. A tall, slender article of furniture, designed for use while shaving. An adjustable mirror of any shape that stands above a small cabinet with compartments to house the straight razor and shaving supplies.
Sideboard. An item of furniture intended for the reception of articles used in the service of the table. Larger in size than a buffet or server.

Spindle. A slender, turned, vertical baluster.
Splashback. A high rim at the back of a washstand to prevent splattering of the wall when using the washbowl.
Stick 'n' ball. A design of spindle work with round balls connected to one another by straight or twisted dowels.
Stool. The simplest seat, which is a chair without a back.
Straight-sawn. Lumber taken from the log by slicing lengthwise, exposing the growth rings of the tree producing straight grain.
T-back. Referring to a chair with a vertical back panel for a "T." Can be plain in many shapes with or without decoration.
Taboret or taborette. A small plant stand.
Tiger-oak. Contemporary name for quartersawn oak graining showing vivid stripes, as a tiger's back.
Top rail. The top member of a chair back; headpiece.
Turning. Shaping wood on a lathe or with chisels to form table or chair legs or spindles.
Upholstered seat. Where the seat and possibly the back are padded.
Veneer. A thin coating of ornamental wood permitting a display of figured grain, not possible otherwise. Veneered furniture represents the highest attainment of the furniture maker's art.

Furniture Makers

The following is a list of companies encountered during this writing:
W. J. Able, address not known.
Atlas Furniture Co., Jamestown, New York.
Baker Office Furniture Co., Pittsburgh, Pennsylvania.
Baker & Co., Allegan, Michigan, makers of furniture.
Bailey Tables™.
Barlow & Kent Co., Urbana, Ohio, manufacturers of wardrobes, cupboards, extension tables, and ladies' desks.
Boling Chair Company, Siler City, North Carolina.
Burt Bros., Philadelphia, Pennsylvania.
Brandt Tables, The Brandt Cabinet Works, Hagerstown, Maryland.
Hobart M. Cable, Piano Company, Chicago, Illinois .
Chicago Chair Co., Chicago, Illinois.
Conewango Furniture Co., Warren, Pennsylvania.
Danner, address unknown.
Dubin Co. Inc., Office Furniture & Equipment, Philadelphia, Pennsylvania, office furniture and equipment.
Empire Case Goods, Jamestown, New York, manufacturers of Perma-Lock Lifetime Construction.
Grand Rapids™.
Globe-Wernieke Co., Cincinnati, Ohio. "Branches or Agencies Everywhere; Patented."
Grand Rapids Manufacturing Co., Grand Rapids, Michigan.
Grand Rapids Refrigerator Co., Grand Rapids, Michigan.
Gunn Bookcase Co., Grand Rapids, Michigan.
Hagerstown Furniture, Hagerstown, Maryland, maker of extension tables, stands, etc.
F. E. Hale Manufacturing Co., Herkimer, New York.
Hale Company, Arlington, Vermont, chair manufacturers.
Hale & Kilburn Manufacturing Co./Makers, Philadelphia, Pennsylvania.
Hartley Manufacturing Co., Chicago, Illinois.
Hartwig & Kemper, Baltimore, Maryland.
Hastings Table Co., Hastings, Michigan.
A. H. Heilman & Co., Williamsport, Pennsylvania.
Heywood Wakefield Company, Chicago, Illinois.
High Furniture Company, High Point, North Carolina.
R. J. Horner, New York, New York.
Humphrey Bookcase Co., Detroit, Michigan.
Hunzinger, address unknown.

Joseph C. Hainey & Sons, Philadelphia, Pennsylvania.
K. C. Co., Chester, Pennsylvania.
Larkin Co., Buffalo, New York.
Lebanon Valley Furniture Co., Lebanon, Pennsylvania, manufacturers of dressers, princess dressers, and chiffoniers.
Library Bureau Solemakers, address unknown.
R. A. Macey & Co., address unknown.
Maceys, address unknown.
Metropolitan Chair Co., New Haven, Connecticut.
Maine Manufacturing Co., Nashua, New Hampshire.
Midland Manufacturing Co., Chicago, Illinois.
D. Y. Mowday, Norristown, Pennsylvania, cabinetmaker.
Michelsen & Hopper, N. Water St., Rochester, New York, manufacturers of furniture.
National Furniture Co., Jamestown, New York, manufacturers of dining room, parlor and library tables, taborets, and pedestals.
Paris Manufacturing Co., address unknown.
Paine Furniture Co. Boston, Massachusetts.
Penn Furniture Co., Philadelphia, Pennsylvania.
J. K. Riskel Furniture, Williamsport, Pennsylvania.
Robbins Table Co., Owosso, Michigan.
Royal Chair Co., Sturgis, Michigan.
Shelbyville Desk Co., Shelbyville Indiana.
Sikes Co., Philadelphia, Pennsylvania.
Sterling Furniture Co., Greensboro, North Carolina.
Star Furniture Co., Jamestown, New York, chamber furniture.
Statesville Furniture Company, Statesville, North Carolina, manufacturers of oak and mahogany suites, odd dressers, chiffoniers, and sideboards.
Technical Supply Co., Sole Manufacturer, Scranton, Pennsylvania.
Tell City Furniture Co., Tell City, Indiana.
Trymby, Hunt , and Co., Philadelphia, Pennsylvania, manufacturers and importers of furniture and decorations.
Van Stee Corp., Jamestown, New York, furniture of distinctive merit.
Watsontown Table & Furniture Co., Watsontown, Pennsylvania.
Webb Furniture Company, Galax, Virginia.
Widman, address unknown.
Wisconsin Chair Company, Port Washington, Wisconsin.
Yawman and Erbe Manufacturing Company, Rochester, New York.

Retail Stores

Ben's Reliable Furniture, Philadelphia, Pennsylvania.
Charles Wilson Stores, New York City.
John Wanamaker, Philadelphia.
Snellenburg's.Market, 11th to 12thST., Philadelphia, Pennsylvania,"The Store for Thrifty People."
Hecht Bros. Co, Baltimore, Maryland.

Bibliography

Century Furniture Company. *Furniture.* Grand Rapids, Michigan: 1928.

Feinman, Jeffrey, ed. *Fall 1909 Sears, Roebuck Catalogue.* New York, New York: Ventura Books, Inc., 1979.

Grow, Lawrence, ed. *The Old House Book of Bedrooms.* New York, New York: The Main Street Press, Warner Books, Inc., 1980.

Grow, Lawrence, ed. *The Old House Book of Living Rooms and Parlors.* New York, New York: The Main Street Press, Warner Books, Inc., 1980.

Israel, Fred L.,ed. *1897 Sears, Roebuck Catalogue.* New York, New York: Chelsea House Publishers, 1976.

"Mercury," Encyclopedia Brittanica, 1958 ed., vol. 8. Chicago.

Schiffer, Nancy N. *America's Oak Furniture.* West Chester, Pennsylvania: Schiffer Publishing Ltd., 1989.

Schroeder, Joseph J., ed. *Fall 1900 Sears, Roebuck and Company Catalogue.* Northfield, Illinois: DBI Books, Inc., Technical Publishing Co., 1970.

Sutcliffe, G. Lester, ed. *The Modern Carpenter Joiner and Cabinet-Maker.* The Modern Carpenter Joiner and Cabinet-Maker Series. The National Historical Society, 1990.

Wanamaker Store, John. *The Wanamaker Diary, 1907.* Philadelphia, Pennsylvania, 1907.